GW01605854

DISCOVER
PARIS

ISABELLE CALABRE

LEARN EVERYTHING THERE IS TO KNOW ABOUT THE CAPITAL!

© 2024
ÉDITIONS
PARIGRAMME /
COMPAGNIE
PARISIENNE DU
LIVRE (PARIS)

IMAGINE

gladiator fights in the
Arènes de Lutèce or life in the
bustling streets of medieval Paris...

UNCOVER

the secrets of the *Mona Lisa*
and the Eiffel Tower...

EXPLORE

fantastic gardens and go looking
for strange animals...

EMBARK

on a trip along the canals
or down in the depths of the metro...

UNDERSTAND

how Rue des Poissonniers and the opera cake
got their names...

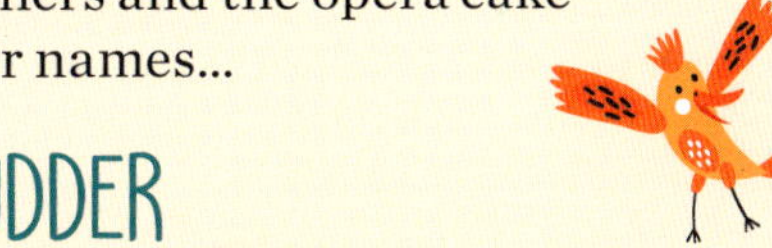

SHUDDER

at the number of rats and pigeons
that swarm the city...
And hunt for ghosts that haunt
our minds and monuments...

...

DISCOVER

Paris through a thousand hilarious facts
and impress your parents with your
knowledge!

CONTENTS!

PREHISTORIC HISTORY

Paris wasn't populated in a day. For proof, look at this mammoth's molar and these remains of jewelry and dugout canoes...

HUNTER-GATHERERS LIVED IN PARIS!

In 2006, under a road in the 15th arrondissement, people discovered traces of hunter-gatherers who lived during the **Mesolithic**, a period that lasted between - 12 500 to - 6 000 BC. They found animal carcasses, remains of shell and bone jewelry, needles for sewing animal skins, buttons... so much precious evidence about our ancestors!

SAILING DOWN THE RIVER...

In 1991, just before former wine storage warehouses were turned into a park, archeologists working on a dig in Bercy found remains of ten **dugout canoes**. These boats were used by fishermen living incamps along the Seine. The oldest one dates back to the Neolithic, which was from - 6 000 to - 3 000 BC.

FIND THE MAMMOTH!

It appears the pachyderm enjoyed living by the Seine. An 8.5-inch **mammoth molar**, currently on display at the Musée Carnavalet, was found under Avenue Daumesnil; another was found under Place de l'Opéra and a whole skeleton was uncovered in Square Montholon. These huge animals lived between - 200 000 and - 13 000 BC at a time when the Parisian basin had a very cold and dry climate. Their meat was one of prehistorical humans' favorite food.

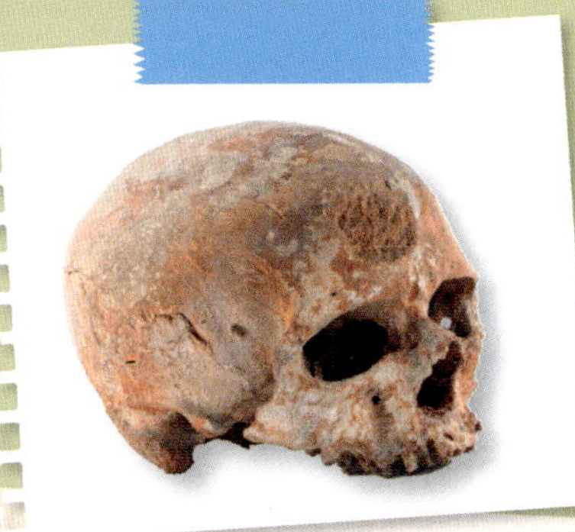

WE FOUND CRO-MAGNON'S SKULL!

It's true that Cro-Magnon was not Parisian since he was discovered in Périgord, in the 19th century, at the bottom of a cave to which he owes his name. This *Homo sapiens* that looked like us lived around 35,000 years ago and was around 40 years old. For his time, he was a really old man. You can admire his skull at the **Musée de l'Homme**, at the Palais de Chaillot.

JURASSIC PARK AT THE JARDIN DES PLANTES

The most terrifying dinosaur skeleton is without a doubt the 27-yard-long **diplodocus** on exhibit in the central aisle of the Galerie de Paléontologie. But the iguanodons and other triceratops aren't bad either! None of these fossils were dug up in Paris, but they have been in the museum's collection since the 19th century.

IN ROMAN TIMES

After conquering Gaul, the Romans settled in Paris—or rather Lutèce—on the left bank, on the Sainte-Geneviève mountain. To be honest, it's more of a hill than a "mountain," but it was sufficient to avoid the floods of the Seine.

ARE YOU COMING TO FIGHT?

A GRID CITY

The Roman engineers in charge of organizing Lutèce first drew up a grid, exactly as they would have done for an army camp with tents lined up in a row. This grid helped them decide where the roads should be, and where to build monuments and houses. They then placed their measuring device, the *groma*, at the highest point (which is now at 172–174 Rue Saint Jacques) and traced the most important road, the **cardo maximus**, which crosses the city from south to north as in all Roman cities. Today, this is Rue Saint Jacques, which descends towards the Seine. From this road, they traced parallel streets and then worked on perpendicular ones, of which the main one (**decumanus maximus**) must have been Rue Cujas.

Model of the forum, in the city center

MEET YOU AT THE FORUM

The most important building in Lutèce was the **forum**. This explains why it was located at the crossroads of the *cardo* and the *decumanus* and overlooks the whole city. The forum was where people met to settle political and administrative matters as well as being the center for business and religion. 195 yards long and 97 yards wide, on the current map, it went from Rue Saint Jacques to Boulevard Saint-Michel. All that's left to see of it is a small piece of wall, when going into the underground parking lot at 63 Boulevard Saint-Michel.

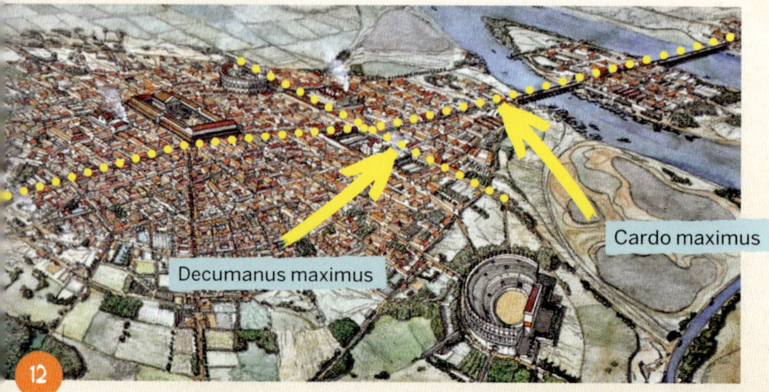

All that remains of the forum...

Musée de Cluny
6 Place Paul-Painlevé
75005 Paris
01 53 73 78 00
musee-moyenage.fr

THE ROMAN LIFESTYLE WAS PRETTY NICE!

People of course washed at the **thermal baths**, but that wasn't all. In this place for relaxation, people spent hours going between cold pools (*frigidarium*), warm rooms (*tepidarium*) and hot pools. They engaged in different sports, had massages, and met with friends. The only baths in Lutèce which survived are the ones visible from outside and inside the **Musée de Cluny.**

The Roman baths at Cluny

A PORT ON THE ÎLE DE LA CITÉ QUAY

The Romans extended the *cardo* with a bridge linking to the Île de la Cité. They built houses, stabilized the banks and set up a port. **Part of one of these quays remains in the archeological crypt of the paved square at Notre-Dame Cathedral**.

Archaeological Crypt on Notre-Dame's square
7 Parvis Notre-Dame
Place Jean-Paul-II
75004 Paris
01 55 42 50 10
crypte.paris.fr

GAMES AND FIGHTING FOR ENTERTAINMENT

An impressive amphitheater allowed 17,000 people to attend plays with singing and dancing as well as fights between ferocious animals or gladiators. The ruins can be found in the **Arènes de Lutèce** gardens.

The Arènes de Lutèce

Arènes de Lutèce
49 Rue Monge
75005 Paris
paris.fr

FROM LUTÈCE TO PARIS, THE BIRTH OF A CAPITAL CITY

In 508, Clovis, king of the Franks, decided to make Paris the capital city. Back then, the town had 30,000 inhabitants—far fewer than Lyon, which was considered the main city of the kingdom.

WHERE DOES THE NAME PARIS COME FROM?

The first Gallic inhabitants of the region belonged to the small Parisii tribe. The Romans who conquered the land called it "Lutèce of the **Parisii**" and by the 4th century it was simply called "Paris." The name "parisii" features in many place names in the Île-de-France region, such as Villeparisis and Cormeilles-en-Parisis.

PROTECT US SAINTE GENEVIÈVE!

The patron saint of Paris was born in 423. She was very devout and became famous in 451 when Paris was under siege by Attila and the Huns. She saved the city by encouraging the residents, especially women, to resist and pray. She then had a church built by Clovis, where she was buried in 512. **All that remains of this church is the bell**, that you can see behind the walls of the Henri-IV high school.

Lycée Henri-IV
23 Rue Clovis
75005 Paris

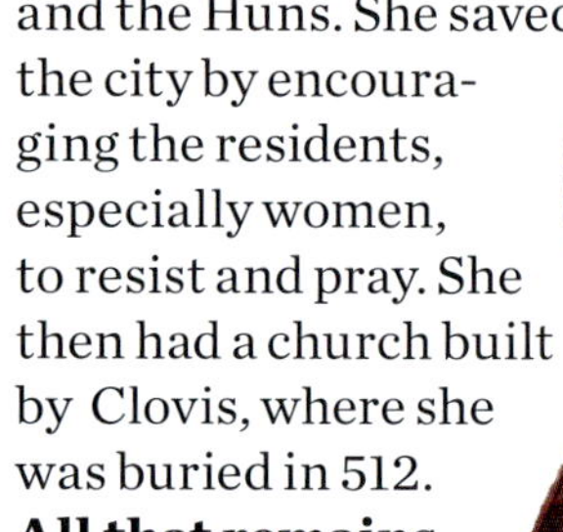

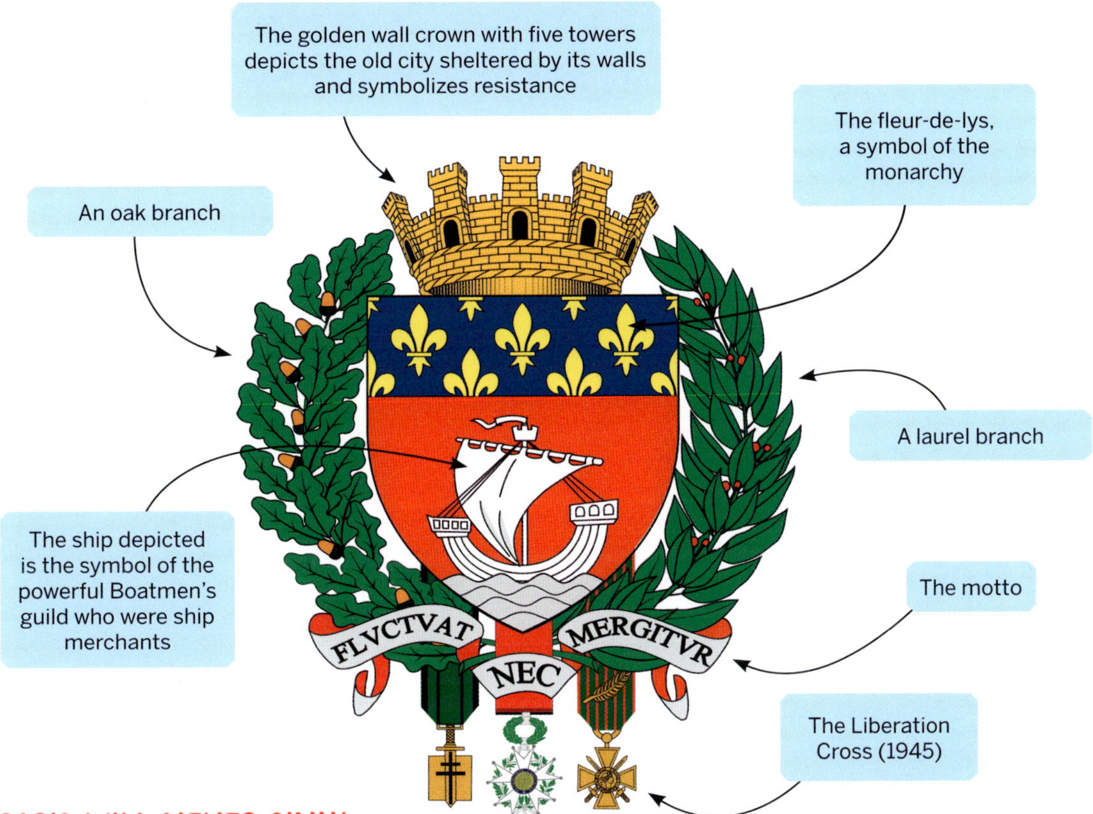

The golden wall crown with five towers depicts the old city sheltered by its walls and symbolizes resistance

The fleur-de-lys, a symbol of the monarchy

An oak branch

A laurel branch

The ship depicted is the symbol of the powerful Boatmen's guild who were ship merchants

The motto

FLVCTVAT NEC MERGITVR

The Liberation Cross (1945)

The Legion of Honor (1900)

The War Cross (1914–1918)

PARIS WILL NEVER SINK!

The Ville de Paris boat's coat of arms is the symbol of the **Nautes guild**, the most powerful guild in Paris during the Antiquity and the Middle Ages. These wealthy merchants organized the transportation of goods along the Seine. They were later authorized to appoint a Provost of Merchants, the precursor to the Mayor of Paris. The Latin motto associated with the coat of arms, "**Fluctuat nec mergitur**" (*He is rocked by the waves but does not sink*), alludes to this river activity. It has become a symbol of the city itself, triumphing over the difficulties and wounds of its history.

The Nautes Pillar

GET YOUR WEAPONS, BOATMEN!

On display in the *frigidarium* of the Cluny thermal baths are fragments of the **Nautes pillar**, discovered beneath the foundations of Notre-Dame. Dating from the Gallo-Roman Lutetia period, this sculpted column was over five yards high; one of its walls depicts the Nautes marching with shields and spears.

Frigidarium of the Musée de Cluny
6 Place Paul-Painlevé
75005 Paris
01 53 73 78 00
musee-moyenage.fr

LIVING IN THE MIDDLE AGES

With 230,000 habitants in the 14th century, the lively, noisy Paris was the most populated city in Europe. Ordinary people, tradesmen and merchants lived in poorly lit rooms and spent most of their days outside. In the Marais district, one of the few that escaped Prefect Haussmann's demolition in the 19th century, you can still see some traces of medieval Paris.

SHELTERED FROM THE RAIN

Dogs, chickens and pigs roamed free in streets lined with craftsmen's and merchants' stalls. An example is **Rue des Barres**, which led from the Seine to the working-class Saint-Gervais district, built on high ground to avoid the marshes along the river's edge. The timber-framed house at nº. 12 has retained its "**jettied**" facade, allowing passers-by to shelter from the rain.

INFURIATING TRAFFIC (ALREADY)

There were no sidewalks in the Middle Ages and for lack of a better solution, Parisians walked in the middle of the road. More often than not, this was a dirt track and not paved. According to city rules, it had to be wide enough to let two carts pass one another... but that wasn't always the case. As for the unlucky pedestrians, they had to watch out for wastewater that could be thrown out of a window at any given moment!

"WATCH OUT FOR THE WATER!"

People used to throw their dirty water or the contents of their chamber pots out the window... To protect passers-by, it was made compulsory to shout: "Watch out for the water" three times before emptying a bucket.

HOUSES THAT AREN'T LIKE THEY MAKE THEM NOW

Narrow and tall, the houses could be four or five stories high. The houses at 11 and 13 **Rue François-Miron** have retained their medieval appearance, even though they've been extensively restored. In the Middle Ages, there was just one room on each floor, into which an entire family was crammed. The stone ground floor was reserved for shops, which opened onto the street and were protected at night by wooden shutters. The facade facing the street is "gabled" (*en pignon* in French), meaning it ends in a triangle topped with a pointed roof. Only the gables of poor people's houses opened onto an alley or a courtyard. The expression "*avoir pignon sur rue*" (to have a gable on the street) thus refers to wealthy people.

PARIS PROTECTED BY RAMPARTS

In 1190, **King Philippe Auguste**, who was leaving for a crusade, had a thick wall built around Paris in order to not leave it undefended. It was three miles long, 30 feet high and ten feet wide, with 77 look-out towers and 17 fortified gates. A 66-yard-long section of the wall remains on **Rue des Jardins-Saint-Paul**.

BEAUTIFUL CHÂTEAUX

In the Middle Ages, the king and his court lived in castles which gradually lost their fortress-like appearance and were transformed into comfortable palaces. The majority were destroyed but some remain... in their own way.

THE TALLEST AND MOST SECURE

Standing at 170 feet high, the square **keep** at **Château de Vincennes** is the tallest in Europe. Built for King Charles V during the Hundred Years' War in the 14th century, it included kitchens, a council chamber, the King's bedroom and an adjoining study. Defended by a drawbridge and fortified walls, it was a safe haven in the event of an English attack.

THE MOST MAJESTIC

At the end of the 13th century, King Philip The Fair transformed the old Palais de la Cité, beside the Seine, into the most splendid royal château in Europe. When it became the **Conciergerie** prison, it retained its fine appearance with its four towers—three round and one square. The first **public clock** in Paris was installed in 1370 on the square tower; since then, it has been restored several times.

THE BEST HIDDEN

All that remains of the Hôtel de Bourgogne, which belonged to John the Fearless, is the 69-foot-high **fortified tower** at 20 **Rue Étienne-Marcel**. John may have been fearless but he dreaded an act of revenge after having had his cousin, the King's brother, murdered in 1407. This tower–which was supposed to protect him– didn't stop him from in turn being killed by his rivals, when his time came, near Fontainebleau in 1419.

THE MOST ELEGANT

Part castle, part palace, with its three pointed-roofed turrets, square keep, Gothic gateway and delicately sculpted windows, the **Hôtel de Sens** was built in the 15th century. It was the residence of the archbishops of Sens, who answered to the bishop of Paris. Today, the property houses a library.

THE RICHEST IN TREASURE

Built in 1485 for the abbot of Cluny, Jacques d'Amboise, the **Hôtel de Cluny** was home to several royal guests, including Queen Mary of England. In the 19th century, it was transformed into a national museum about the Middle Ages, housing sculptures, tapestries, weapons, and objects made of gold, silver, ivory, and rare woods... sometimes covered in enamel or precious stones.

Château de Vincennes
Avenue de Paris
94300 Vincennes
01 48 08 31 20
chateau-de-vincennes.fr

Conciergerie
2 Boulevard du Palais
75001 Paris
01 53 40 60 80
paris-conciergerie.fr

Tour Jean-sans-Peur
20 Rue Étienne-Marcel
75002 Paris
01 40 26 20 28

Hôtel de Sens (Bibliothèque Forney)
1 Rue du Figuier
75004 Paris
01 42 78 14 60
paris.fr/lieux/bibliotheque-forney-18

Musée de Cluny
6 Place Paul-Painlevé
75005 Paris
01 53 73 78 00
musee-moyenage.fr

SAINTE-CHAPELLE,
TREASURE AND STAINED-GLASS WINDOWS

Sainte-Chapelle was built to house relics purchased by King Louis IX, the future Saint Louis, from the Emperor of Constantinople: the crown of thorns worn by Jesus at the time of his crucifixion, a piece of the cross on which he died, the spear that pierced his side, and the sponge that wiped his forehead. Since 1806, the crown has been kept in a safe in Notre-Dame Cathedral in Paris.

Buttress

A VERY EXPENSIVE CROWN

Supposedly woven 1,200 years earlier, in the 12th century, the crown of thorns was described as still green and soft to the touch, a sign of its holiness... Saint Louis considered it valuable enough to buy it for **135,000 livres**, which was more than half the kingdom's annual income! When the crown arrived in France on August 19, 1239, the king stripped off his luxurious clothes, donned a simple tunic and wore the crown himself, walking barefoot to Notre-Dame Cathedral. It would remain there until the Sainte-Chapelle was ready ready to receive it.

The crown of thorns

A RAPID CONSTRUCTION

The architect of this **Gothic masterpiece** was probably Pierre de Montreuil, who also worked on Notre-Dame de Paris and Saint-Denis Cathedral. The Sainte-Chapelle was built between 1241 and 1248, in record time given the difficulties involved: in order to leave as much room as possible for the stained glass windows, and to achieve the impression of extreme airiness and elevation that we feel when inside, the structure had to be supported by massive buttresses, which are visible from the outside.

Saint Louis receiving the Holy Crown, the Holy Cross, the Holy Spear, and other relics, illumination from the 14th century.

A FLOOR FOR EACH CLASS!

Courtiers and people in service to the king came to pray in the **lower chapel**, with its magnificent painted vault. Only the sovereign and his family had privileged access to the **upper chapel**, where the relics were formerly stored, and they could admire the religious scenes represented on the enormous 52-foot-high glass windows.

The upper chapel

The lower chapel

STAINED-GLASS WINDOWS

The composition of stained-glass windows is made up of pieces of white and colored glass, assembled with lead rods which create the scene.

ONE HELL OF A COMIC STRIP!

The **stained-glass windows** at Sainte-Chapelle are world famous. Just like a comic strip, they depict various events from the Bible. Of the 1,113 panels in the composition, 713 are originals dating back to the building's construction.

Sainte-Chapelle
8 Boulevard du Palais
75001 Paris
01 53 40 60 80
sainte-chapelle.fr

THE LOUVRE, SO MUCH HISTORY!

Before becoming a museum, the Louvre was the palace for the French kings. It all began in 1190, when Philippe Auguste had a fortress built to defend Paris. Two centuries later, Charles V transformed it into a residence worthy of a king and set up his library in one of the towers. Francis I and his son Henri II then turned it into a Renaissance castle. Each sovereign that followed embellished the building in their own way.

Remains of Philippe Auguste's keep

WHAT REMAINS OF THE FORTRESS?

When following the **medieval Louvre** tour, you walk alongside the base of the 12th-century rectangular outer wall, which had King Philippe Auguste's keep at the center.

Model of the castle under Charles V

RECORD FIGURES!

The Louvre palace has:

- 403 rooms
- 2,615,630 sq. ft. of floor space
- 9 miles of corridors
- 10,000 steps
- 410 windows
- 3,000 locks

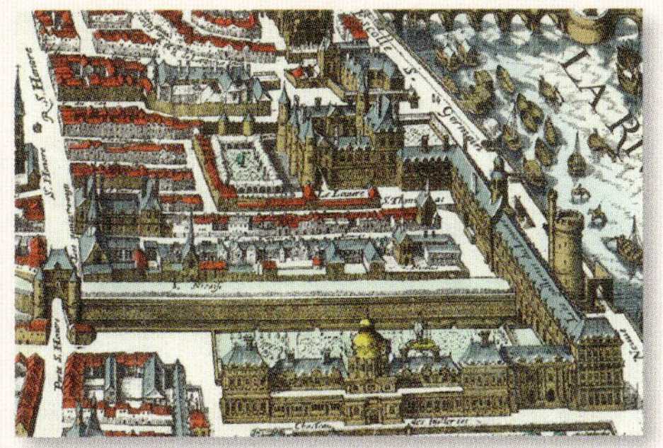

TREASURES... FOR THE PEOPLE

In 1793, during the French Revolution, part of the Louvre palace was redesigned as a museum so that people could admire the treasures the kings had amassed. But it was **Napoleon I** who really established the museum, opening new rooms and filling them with the works of art he had taken from the countries his armies had defeated.

A STYLE FOR EACH KING

From the days of Francis I to Louis XIV's reign, the Louvre quadrupled in size. To see this, you need to stand in the **Cour Carrée**. Just below, in the southwestern quarter to be exact, is the **medieval Louvre**, as seen inside the museum. Francis I and Henri II had half of the wing, which now separates the Cour Carrée from the Cour Napoleon, built in the **Renaissance** style, according to plans by architect Pierre Lescot. Henri IV built the **Galerie au Bord de l'Eau**. Louis XIV commissioned architect Claude Perrault, the brother of the author of the famous fairytales, to close the Cour carrée with a large **colonnade** overlooking Rue de l'Amiral-de-Coligny. The **facade on Rue de Rivoli**, decorated with busts of generals, was started by Napoleon I and completed by Napoleon III.

ONE PYRAMID, TWO PYRAMIDS...

The Chinese-born American architect Ieoh Ming Pei was chosen by President François Mitterrand to design a new entrance to the museum, in the center of the Cour Napoleon. Inaugurated in 1989, the **Louvre pyramid** is composed of 600 rhombuses and 70 triangles of transparent glass. It has four smaller replicas: three "pyramidons" in each corner and an inverted pyramid under the courtyard.

Henri IV

Louis XIV

I MADE THE COLONNADE!

Napoleon I

GUYS, I'VE GOT AN IDEA! WHAT IF WE TURNED IT INTO A MUSEUM?

Napoleon III

AND VOILÀ! CONSTRUCTION IS FINISHED!

MASTERPIECES GALORE

The Louvre museum houses almost 500,000 works of art from every continent. Many lie dormant in warehouses, and sheltered from daylight; only 38,000 are on display to the public. Among them are a few stars...

THE VENUS DE MILO OR THE IDEAL WOMAN

According to ancient beauty standards, the face and body of this marble statue from the 1st century BC epitomize the ideal woman. Hence the name Venus, the Roman name for the goddess of beauty. As for Milo, that's the name of the Greek island where the statue was discovered in 1820.

THE SEATED SCRIBE, THE DISTINGUISHED EGYPTIAN

Scribes, who were both private secretaries and administrative officials, were important people in the days of the pharaohs. Like the majority of works around it, this statue comes from the former Egyptian museum. It was founded at the Louvre by Champollion, the hieroglyph decipherer, to collect the treasures brought back from Egypt by Napoleon Bonaparte in 1802.

IN THE WIND: THE WINGED VICTORY OF SAMOTHRACE

It personifies victory, which, for the Greeks, is always winged. 2,200 years ago, it adorned a Greek temple facing the Aegean Sea, next to which it was found in pieces in 1863. Its boat-shaped base indicates that it was celebrating a naval victory; you can almost feel the wind ripping through its wings...

Musée du Louvre
99 Rue de Rivoli
75001 Paris
01 40 20 50 50
louvre.fr

THE WEDDING AT CANA, A RECORD-BREAKING PAINTING

Measuring 23 feet high and 33 feet wide with 130 figures, this painting by Veronese, an Italian Renaissance painter, is the biggest in the Louvre.

THE EMPEREROR'S CORONATION, BEST DONE HIMSELF...

On this enormous canvas, the painter David depicted the ceremony on December 2, 1804 when Napoleon Bonaparte crowned himself emperor of the French, and then crowned his wife Joséphine.

THE RAFT OF THE MEDUSA, THE SYMBOL OF ALL SHIPWRECKS

This shipwreck scene painted in 1818 by Théodore Géricault represents a historic event: of the 147 people who escaped from the ship *La Méduse*, only 15 survived, the others having died of hunger, thirst... or cannibalism!

DO YOU WANT TO DISCOVER MY MASTERPIECE? TURN TO THE NEXT PAGE!

LEONARDO

THE MONA LISA,
THE MOST FAMOUS PAINTING IN THE WORLD

Painted by Leonardo Da Vinci at the very start of the 16th century, the *Mona Lisa* was purchased by Francis I. For a long time, it was kept in the royal collection until Napoleon Bonaparte moved it into the brand new Louvre museum for everyone to see.

PRETTY WOMAN OR HOLY VIRGIN?

A pretty woman is sitting on the balcony of an Italian abode; behind her we can make out a landscape of gently rolling hills under the northern Italian sky. Her attitude makes her look like the **Virgin**, as if it were a religious painting. It was quite daring at the time!

WATCH OUT, VANDALS!

In 1911, Vincenzo Perruggia, an Italian employee at the Louvre, believed that the painting had been unjustly stolen by Francis I almost four centuries earlier and wanted to return it to his home country. He stole it from the Louvre, which caused a **worldwide scandal**. The *Mona Lisa* was found three years later and returned to the museum after the incredible incident which contributed to its popularity. There was more excitement in 1957, when a visitor tried to throw a stone at the painting. For a few years now it has been covered by a thick layer of glass protection so it's no longer at risk!

ARTFUL BLURRING

It's the **sfumato** effect, a technique Leonardo invented and which was much admired by his contemporaries. Thanks to the layering of dozens of very thin layers of transparent paint, the silhouette's contours seem to melt into the landscape, giving it depth and an incredible softness.

WHO WAS MONNA LISA?

Her French name "La Joconde" derives from Francesco del Giocondo, an Italian merchant. The young woman was supposedly his **wife**, Lisa. "Monna" is the abbreviation of *madonna*, which means "madam" in Italian.

L.H.O.O.Q.

In 1920, the artist **Marcel Duchamp**, specialized in reinterpretations and provocation, caused a scandal (intentionally!) when he made this reproduction of the *Mona Lisa*. When you read the letters in the caption aloud in French, it sounds a lot like "She has a hot ass!"

NOTRE-DAME, A LEGENDARY CATHEDRAL

In the Middle Ages, people traveling to Paris could see the cathedral's silhouette from very far away as it towered over the rooftops. But once they got into the city, it was another matter. The paved square in front of it used to be a lot smaller than it is today, the roads were very narrow, and it was only at the last moment, when turning a corner, that people suddenly discovered the cathedral. Dramatic effect guaranteed!

SCARY UGLY: THE GARGOYLES

Their deformed appearance is meant to ward off demons. But **gargoyles** mainly have a practical role: by extending out the gutters, they drain rainwater away from the walls, protecting them from seepage. These ones were designed by the architect Viollet-le-Duc in the 19th century. Between the two towers, he also created the fantastic half-human, half-animal sculptures in the **Chimera Gallery**.

Viollet-le-Duc

VIOLLET-LE-DUC, NOTRE-DAME'S SAVIOR

Jean de Chelles and Pierre de Montreuil built the cathedral in the 13th and 14th centuries. But after the Revolution and years of neglect, Notre-Dame was in a very bad state; it was thanks to the novel by Victor Hugo, *Notre-Dame de Paris*, published in 1831, that people took interest in it again and the decision was made to restore it. The architect **Viollet-le-Duc** was in charge of the project... even adding details of his own invention to make the cathedral look even more Gothic. And he gave the statue of the apostle Saint Thomas his own face, as he contemplates the spire on the roof that he has just rebuilt.

ALL ROADS LEAD TO PARIS

In front of the paved square at Notre-Dame, a bronze plaque with a six-point star marks **kilometer zero**, which is the exact point from which all distances between the capital and the rest of the country are calculated.

EMMANUEL, THE TENOR BELL

A tenor bell is a large bell with a deep sound. The first one to be installed at Notre-Dame, in 1400, answered to the pretty name Jacqueline. It was melted down in the 17th century to create the **Emmanuel tenor bell**, named after Louis XIV's grandson. Before switching to electricity, it took 16 men to make this 14-ton bell move with pedals. In 2013 it was joined by the Marie tenor bell.

KINGS OR REVOLUTIONARIES?

Above the three doorways on the main facade, the Gallery of Kings shows 28 statues of the **kings of Judah** all in a line, who are considered to be the Virgin Mary's ancestors. But, during the Revolution, the *sans-culottes* (French revolutionaries) thought they were the kings of France, who they hated: so the statues were destroyed and no more was said about them. In the 19th century, Viollet-le-Duc remade statues for the gallery and this time... he included himself in the eighth statue on the left. While he was at it, he also featured two of his coworkers! There was a dramatic turnaround in 1977 when 21 heads of the destroyed statues were found buried in a mansion's courtyard in the 9th arrondissement. They had been there for almost 200 years. Today, they are on display at the Musée de Cluny.

On April 15, 2019, a terrible fire burnt down the roof and spire of the cathedral. After essential structural repair work, the renovation of the building began. More than 1,000 oak trees have been cut down to rebuild the roof structure, and a quarry in the Oise region is supplying the stones to be replaced on the facade. It is hoped that Notre-Dame will be able to reopen to the public in spring 2024.

Cathédrale Notre-Dame de Paris
6 Parvis Notre-Dame
75004 Paris
notredamedeparis.fr

PAGODAS, MOSQUES, HUTS
AND OTHER TEMPLES

With around a hundred Parisian churches, Catholicism is the most prominent religion in the capital. But people practice many other faiths in Paris, each with unique and sometimes surprising places of worship.

LA GRANDE MOSQUÉE, AN ORIENTAL AIR

Founded in 1926, the **Grande Mosquée** in Paris was the first mosque to be built in France. The 108-foot-high minaret, which calls believers to prayer, as well as the patio, colorful mosaics and marble columns in the main courtyard, are inspired by North-African mosques, on the other side of the Mediterranean.

Grande Mosquée de Paris
2 bis Place du Puits-de-l'Ermite
75005 Paris
01 45 35 97 33
mosqueedeparis.net

AN AFRICAN HUT STYLE BUDDHIST PAGODA

This pagoda, built in the former Cameroon Pavillion from the 1931 Colonial Exhibition in the Bois de Vincennes, looks more like a giant African hut than an Asian temple. Worshippers gather around a 29.5-foot-high **Buddha** covered in gold leaf. It is the tallest one in Europe.

Grande Pagode
40 bis Route de ceinture du lac Daumesnil
75012 Paris
01 43 41 02 49

CELEBRATING GANESH

Every August, a big procession sets off from France's largest hindu temple, **Vinayakar Alayam**, which is near Boulevard de la Chapelle, to celebrate the elephant-headed god **Ganesh's** birthday. His golden statue parades through the streets on a float decorated with flowers, escorted by dancers and musicians in traditional costumes and followed by thousands of Hindus and other curious individuals.

Temple Vinayakar Alayam
17 Rue Pajol
75018 Paris
01 40 34 21 89
templeganesh.fr

Jardin d'Acclimatation
Bois de Boulogne
75116 Paris
01 40 67 90 85
jardindacclimatation.fr

A ZEN GARDEN FOR MEDITATION

Since 2002, the **Jardin de Séoul**, inside the Jardin d'Acclimatation, has brought together the symbols of Korean ancestral traditions across its 5,980-square yard-site, in keeping with the principles inherited from the Chinese sage Confucius. Wooden houses with thatched roofs, a sacred ginkgo tree, a purifying pool, and the Gate of Paradise provide a space for meditation.

A HUT IN WHICH TO PRAY AND REMEMBER

In addition to several synagogues, some of which date back to the 19th century, the **Musée d'Art et d'Histoire du Judaïsme** in the Marais district is home to an original and rare hut. In this temporary shelter, with its roof covered in branches and foliage, Eastern-European practicing Jews would spend a week during the fall harvest festival of Sukkot, remembering the wandering of their people during the Exodus.

Musée d'Art et d'Histoire du judaïsme
71 Rue du Temple
75003 Paris
01 53 01 86 53
mahj.org

HÔTEL DES INVALIDES,
A KING'S GIFT TO HIS SOLDIERS

In 1671, Louis XIV created this large complex of buildings for the elderly, disabled and homeless soldiers in his armies. The institution, the only one of its kind in the world at the time, has now been transformed into the fascinating Musée de l'Armée. It is still home to a number of military residents.

HOSPITAL OR RETIREMENT HOME ?

In the 17th century, the Invalides had two functions. While some soldiers were cared for in the infirmary, each in their own bed—a rare luxury at the time—others were simply housed and fed all year round, which meant they didn't have to beg in the streets. Initially designed for **2,000 boarders**, the Hôtel des Invalides grew to house 4,000 people by 1714.

LOUVOIS THE WOLF

The Secretary of State for War, the Marquis de **Louvois**, carried out the King's wishes. He would have liked to leave his mark on Les Invalides, but Louis XIV wanted to be the only one represented on the building's facade—as an emperor on horseback, on top of the central pavilion. Instead, Louvois had a wolf discreetly carved on a dormer window in the main courtyard to represent himself, with "loup voit", meaning "the watching wolf", sounding a lot like his name "Louvois."

Marquis de Louvois

MINIATURE CITIES TO PLAY WARGAMES

The attic of the Hôtel des Invalides houses the Musée des **Plans-reliefs**. Produced in the 17th century, these 1:600 scale models of fortified towns such as Belfort, Perpignan and Lille were used to train for sieges and defenses.

SHOOT THE CANNONS, GREET THE PRESIDENT!

The superb cannons seized from enemies and lined up on the esplanade are not there simply to impress passers-by. Every five years, these **historic artillery pieces** are deployed and fire 21 empty rounds to celebrate the inauguration of the new President of the Republic.

I'M PRESIDENT OF THE REPUBLIC!!

TREASURE AT THE TOP

The top of the domed church is covered with 550,000 leaves of pure gold, equivalent to 26 pounds of gold.

WAHOO!

TWEET TWEET!

TWEET TWEET

Invalides - Musée de l'Armée
129 Rue de Grenelle
75007 Paris
01 44 42 38 77
musee-armee.fr

HERE LIES NAPOLEON

The emperor, who died in exile in St. Helena in 1821, wanted to be laid to rest "on the banks of the Seine." 19 years after his dying wish, Napoleon's remains were returned by the British and repatriated to France. Since then, 12 angel statues have watched over the **imperial tomb** beneath the dome of the royal church.

REVOLUTIONARY RENDEZVOUS

Revolution Paris isn't limited to Place de la Bastille. Other locations were the settings of important events and certain monuments commemorate them.

A CAFÉ BUZZING WITH NEW IDEAS

At 13 Rue de l'Ancienne-Comédie, the oldest café in Paris, **The Procope**, welcomed Danton, Robespierre and Marat–famous revolutionaries on numerous occasions. In the window displays and on the walls inside, you can still see souvenirs from this period.

A ROYAL PALACE OR A REVOLUTIONARY ONE?

Even though the **Palais-Royal** belonged to Louis XVI's cousin, Philippe d'Orléans, it was a hub for political activity. Lots of discussions took place in the cafés and restaurants in the galleries surrounding the gardens–especially since the police weren't allowed to patrol the area. On July 12, 1789, the young lawyer Camille Desmoulins stood on a table and called the crowd to arms. Two days later the storming of the Bastille took place. After the fall of the monarchy in 1792, the Palais-Royal was renamed Palais Égalité (Equality Palace).

REMEMBERING DANTON

Danton's statue is close to the **Cour du Commerce Saint-André** where he lived, a stone's throw away from the School of Medicine, where his friends at the Club des Cordeliers had debates and not far from the Palais du Luxembourg, where he was imprisoned before being guillotined in 1794.

A CHAMBER FOR THE DEPUTIES

At the beginning of the Revolution, the members of parliament held sessions in Versailles. Then, they used an indoor riding academy, near the Tuileries Palace, while the king himself was being brought back from Versailles. In 1793, they set up in the Machines room at the Tuileries theater, which could seat up to 1,500 people. In 1795, they moved to the **Palais Bourbon**, which was renamed the Assemblée Nationale.

THE ARISTOCRATS IN PRISON! THE QUEEN IN THE DUNGEON!

At one point or another during the Revolution, 3,000 aristocrats and political opponents stayed in the largest prison in Paris, the **Conciergerie**. Most of them piled up in the vast Gens d'armes room, but some of the "lucky" ones had private cells, like Marie-Antoinette, whose cell has been reconstructed.

Le Procope
13 Rue de l'Ancienne-Comédie
75006 Paris
01 40 46 79 00
procope.com

Conciergerie
2 Boulevard du Palais
75001 Paris
01 53 40 60 80
paris-conciergerie.fr

I MUST RUN TO THE ASSEMBLÉE!

THE DIABOLICAL GUILLOTINE

The head-cutting machine was installed outside, so that revolutionary executions could be seen by everybody. It was on **Place de la Concorde**, in front of an enormous crowd, that Louis XVI was guillotined on January 21, 1793, followed by Queen Marie-Antoinette in October among many others. The guillotine also fell on Place du Carrousel and Place du Trône, renamed "Place du Trône Renversé" (Overthrown Throne Square); today it's Place de la Nation.

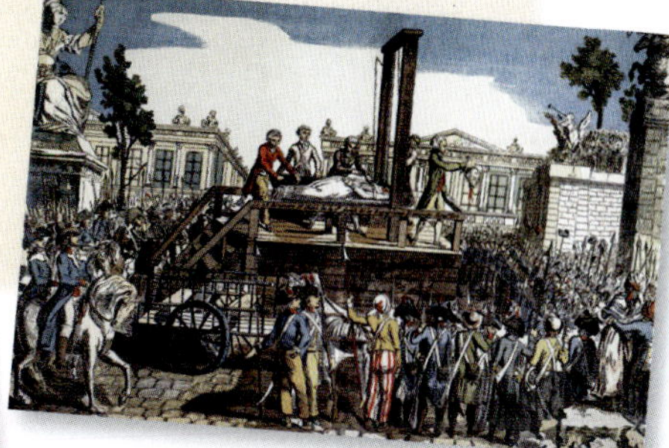

MINI BASTILLE

As soon as the **Bastille** prison had been overthrown, its demolition began: no one wanted to see this sad symbol of the Ancien Régime. But a smart entrepreneur, Pierre-François Palloy, salvaged the stones to use on construction sites around the capital, as well as to make souvenir models of the fortress. One of these is preserved at the Musée Carnavalet.

GLORIOUS STORIES ABOUT THE ARC DE TRIOMPHE

In ancient times, the Romans celebrated their victories by parading their armies under huge archways. Following their example, Napoleon I promised his soldiers who had returned home victorious from the battle of Austerlitz: "You will only return to your homes under arches of triumph!" He ordered the construction of the arch on Place l'Etoile and laid the first stone on August 15, 1806.

THE EMPEROR'S MISSED OPPORTUNITY

When Napoleon married Marie-Louise of Austria in 1810, the monument was just starting to take shape. However, as the Emperor insisted on passing under "his" arch to mark the occasion, a mock-up was built in wood and canvas, like a **life-size model**. Napoleon never actually saw the Arc de Triomphe, as the monument was not inaugurated until 1836, 15 years after his death. However, his coffin, brought back from the island of St. Helena in 1840, would solemnly pass under the arch, carried on a gilded chariot, before being placed in the Invalides.

THE INCREDIBLE FEAT OF AN AVIATION GENIUS

Pilots, who were the heroes of WWI, were outraged to learn that they would be marching on foot in the parade on July 14, 1919, one year after the Armistice, like mere infantrymen. To protest, one of them, **Charles Godefroy**, took the crazy gamble of flying his plane under the Arc de Triomphe. He managed this feat despite the fact that the arch was only 47 feet wide, leaving him a space of just 6.5 feet on either side of his wings.

A TOMB FOR ALL THE UNKNOWN SOLDIERS

We don't know the names of many of the soldiers who were killed during WWI. That's why an anonymous coffin was chosen to represent and commemorate the one and half million Frenchmen who died on the front line between 1914 and 1918. The **unknown soldier** has rested under a granite tombstone at the bottom of the arch since January 28, 1921.

IN HONOR OF FRANCE'S SOLDIERS

At the top of the Arc's pillars, a gigantic 450-foot-long **sculpted band** depicts the armies of the Revolution and the Empire: cavalrymen, hussars and grenadiers, victors of the Egyptian and Italian campaigns.

AN ETERNAL FLAME

The **"flame or remembrance"** burns in tribute to the victims of all wars. Since November 11, 1923, it has never been extinguished. Every evening at 6:30 pm, it is rekindled by veterans' associations to the sound of bugles and drums.

LET'S GO, CHILDREN OF THE NATION...

With wings on her back, the woman sculpted on the right pillar represents **Liberty flying to help the Revolution**. She leads the volunteers defending France against its enemies. From her wide-open mouth, you can hear the words of the of the *Marseillaise*, the French national anthem, which gives its name to this bas-relief sculpted by François Rude.

...THE DAY OF GLORY HAS ARRIVED...

A MONUMENT FROM EGYPT: THE LUXOR OBELISK

At the center of the Place de la Concorde, the Obelisk is the oldest monument in Paris, being over 3,000 years old. In the days of the Pharaohs, it adorned the entrance to the temple in the city of Luxor. It was offered to France in 1830 by Mehemet Ali, Viceroy of Egypt. But it was up to the French to go and get it...

A VERY CUMBERSOME MONUMENT...

The expedition organized by the French to recover the gift from Mehemet Ali involved digging a canal in Egypt to get as close as possible to the monument, and building a special ship, *Le Louxor*, that was capable of carrying the **250-ton** Obelisk. Leaving Toulon in 1831, the ship returned two years later loaded with its precious cargo and reached Paris in August 1834, sailing up the Seine from Le Havre. It took another two years for the Obelisk to reach the center of the Place de la Concorde. The story of this long journey is told in images engraved on the base of the Obelisk.

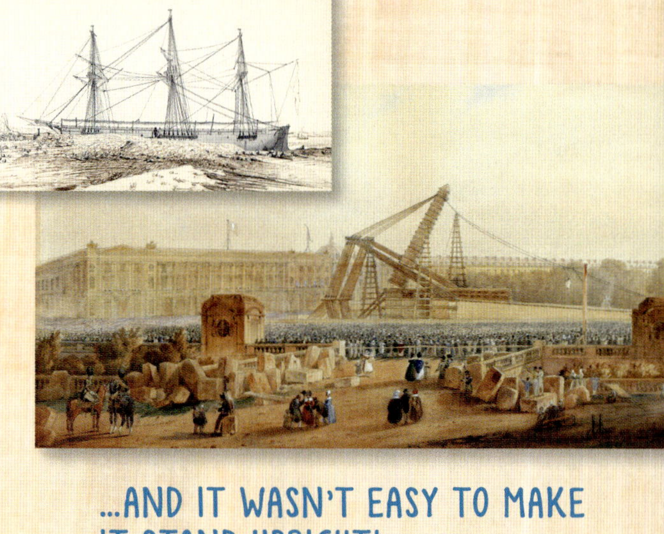

...AND IT WASN'T EASY TO MAKE IT STAND UPRIGHT!

As if it wasn't enough to bring this large block of granite to its final destination, it also had to be made to stand upright. On October 25, 1836, a huge crowd gathered on the Place de la Concorde to witness the event. 300 soldiers and sailors were mobilized to operate **enormous winches** whose ropes were attached to the Obelisk, which slowly but surely reached its upright position. There was a huge round of applause! King Louis-Philippe also witnessed the proceedings, but prudently from a balcony at the Hôtel de la Marine at the far end of the square. He didn't want to have a front-row seat if the operation failed.

Obélisque de Louxor
Place de la Concorde
75008 Paris

DRAWN SCRIPT

Egyptian hieroglyphic script is figurative: its characters represent a variety of objects—natural or man-made—such as plants, figures of gods, humans and animals...

This is how you write PARIS :

P A R I S

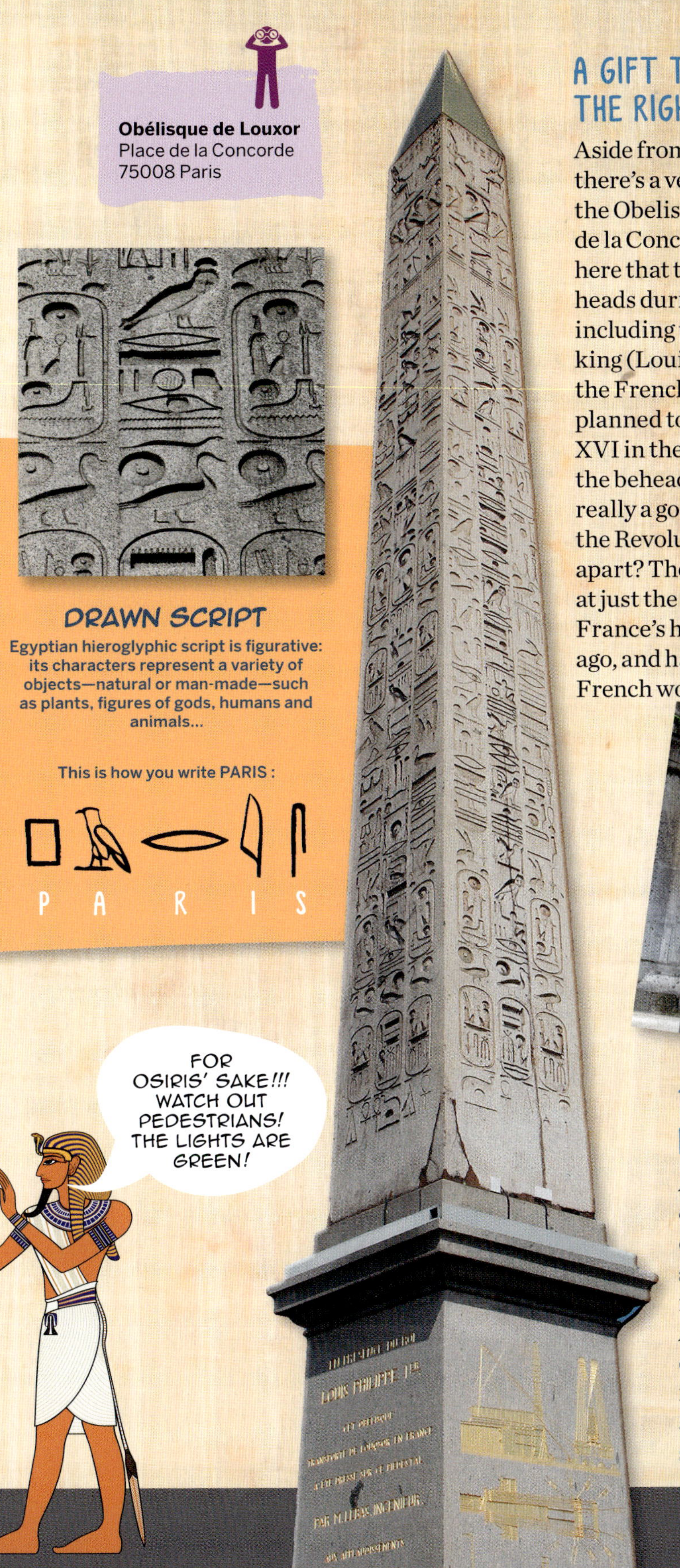

A GIFT THAT CAME AT JUST THE RIGHT TIME

Aside from a love for antiquity, there's a very specific reason why the Obelisk was erected on Place de la Concorde. Don't forget, it was here that the **guillotine** cut off many heads during the French Revolution, including that of Louis XVI. Later, a king (Louis XVIII) was restored to the French throne. The regime then planned to install a statue of Louis XVI in the square to pay homage to the beheaded sovereign. But was it really a good idea to remind people of the Revolution that tore the country apart? The gift from the Nile came at just the right moment. After all, France's history with Egypt was long ago, and had nothing to do with old French wounds...

THEN EGYPT BECAME FASHIONABLE...

At the beginning of the 19th century, Napoleon's military campaigns and Champollion's **study of hieroglyphics** made Egypt all the rage. Architecture, furniture, clothes and hairstyles took inspiration from the country and this ancient civilization swept Parisians off their feet.

THE MOST BEAUTIFUL AVENUE IN THE WORLD: THE CHAMPS-ÉLYSÉES

This avenue is considered the most beautiful in Paris, if not the world, because it stretches out, wide and straight, between the Arc de Triomphe and the Place de la Concorde and is lined with luxury stores. It is often chosen as the location for parades and celebrations.

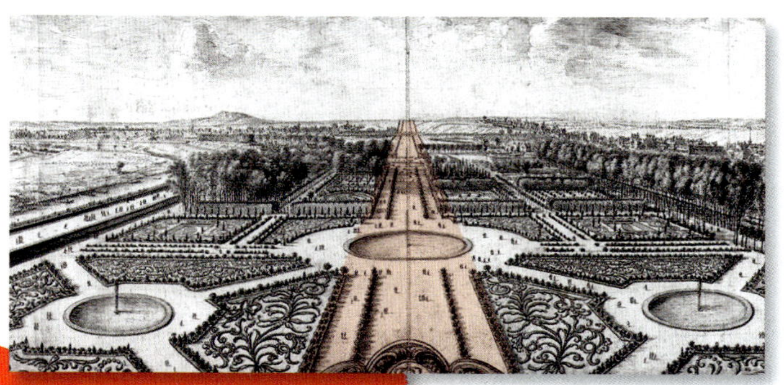

The historic road as seen from the Tuileries Gardens, mapped out to the west by André Le Nôtre.

WELL DONE, LE NÔTRE!

It was Louis XIV's landscape gardener, André Le Nôtre, who mapped out this grand avenue **in the middle of the countryside**. During the French Revolution, it was a popular place for strolling, even though it had little to offer other than a few cafés. It was in the 19th century that the Champs-Élysées really became fashionable, with theaters, concert halls and restaurants. In 1938, the avenue was the first to see its cobblestones covered with tarmac, which made driving much more comfortable.

IT'S CELBRATION TIME!

From sporting events to historical celebrations, people meet on the Champs-Élysées for all big occasions: on New Year's Eve, to celebrate France's victory in the football World Cup, and on August 26, 1944 for the **Liberation of Paris**, when General de Gaulle marched down the avenue surrounded by a million Parisians.

WHAT A FUNNY NAME!

In Greek mythology, it's the name of the part of the underworld where heroes and good people go, to finally enjoy some well-deserved rest... A real slice of heaven where it's spring all year round!

THE END OF THE TOUR

Since 1975, the Champs-Élysées has welcomed cyclists arriving from the world's most famous bike race, the **Tour de France**. But it's not necessarily the easiest part: competitors must loop several times around a a circuit that includes the avenue, before crossing the finish line at the Champs-Élysées roundabout.

LIGHTS!

Every year, on New Year's Eve, tourists and Parisians watch and enjoy a wonderful light show on the Champs-Élysées.

WE'RE HERE TO SEE THE PARADE...

Every **July 14**, during the national holiday, soldiers, police officers and even firefighters march down the Champs-Élysées to reach an official platform set up on Place de la Concorde. There, they greet the President of the Republic, members of government and foreign ambassadors. At the same time, pilots from the airforce perform flight displays above the avenue.

MORE CHIC THAN THE CAR SHOW

If **car companies** have their storefronts on the Champs-Élysées, it's mainly because of the avenue's prestige. But also because they naturally replaced, around 1900, the businesses dealing in horses, carriages and coaches that had set up shop there in the 19th century, as it was the road taken by wealthy Parisians to go for a stroll in the Bois de Boulogne.

THE EIFFEL TOWER, A GLOBAL ICON

Standing at 354 yards high, including its radio and television antennas, it is currently the tallest tower in France and the European Union. In the event of strong winds or extreme heat, the top can bend up to 7 inches. But don't worry, Gustave Eiffel planned for it to be ableto bend up to 27 inches!

AN IMPORTANT SYMBOL!

The Eiffel Tower was completed in 1889, after just two years of construction in time for the Paris **Universal Exposition** celebrating the centenary of the French Revolution.

SAVED THANKS TO ITS ANTENNA

Gustave Eiffel's plan was to build the tallest monument in the world. Mission accomplished: the "300-meter tower," as it was known then, held the record until 1929, when it was beaten by the New York skyscrapers. But with no real use beyond its architectural prowess, the plan was to dismantle it after 20 years. In 1903, however, Eiffel had the idea of attaching a **telegraph antenna** to the top of the tower. Nobody really believed in it... until the First World War, when the tower picked up messages sent by the enemy. From then on, there was no question of the Eiffel Tower disappearing, and once peace had been restored, it became a gigantic antenna for radio and then television broadcasting.

FUNNY MECHANICS

Like a toy construction set, the tower is made up of **18,000 iron pieces** assembled by **2,500,000 metal rivets**. Firmly anchored in their foundations up to 36 feet below ground, its four pillars are linked by two platforms, which form the first and second floors, before meeting on the third floor. The whole structure weighs 11,023 tons.

THE TOWER OF RECORDS

- In 1905, Forestier, winner of the first "stairs championship" walked up to the first floor in 3 minutes and 12 seconds and won... a bicycle!
- In 1944, the American pilot William Overstreet Jr flew through the archway onboard his fighter jet.
- In 1987, A.J. Hackett did a 377-foot bungee jump from the second floor.
- In 2010, Taïg Khris set off from the first floor on roller skates.
- In 2016, the Polish man Piotr Lobodzinski climbed the stairs to the top in 7 minutes and 48 seconds.

MILLIONS OF VISITORS

In the very first week it opened, in May 1889, 30,000 people set out to get to the top, even though the elevators hadn't yet been installed. Since then, **250 million tourists** have come from all over the world.

SHALL WE GO TO THE GIFT SHOP AFTERWARDS?

CRAZY STATISTICS!

354 yards high

1,665 steps to reach the top

300,000 square yards of surface to paint

64,000 miles traveled by the elevators in one year, which is 2.5 times the Earth's circumference!

120 antennas

336 projectors to light it up

20,000 lightbulbs to make it sparkle on the hour, from nightfall until 1 am

A VILLAGE OF PAINTERS: MONTMARTRE

In the 19th century, Montmartre was still a village. Many painters were attracted by theaffordable housing that they could convert into studios. In the evenings, they frequented the district's many cabarets, forming what came to be known as the "Bohemian Montmartre."

A HAVEN FOR GENIUSES

At the beginning of the 20th century, the **Bateau-Lavoir** (meaning "washhouse") was a building divided into artists' studios, housing Juan Gris, Amedeo Modigliani and the man who would become the most famous of them all: Pablo Picasso. Why did it have this strange name? We don't know exactly. Perhaps it's because the building, shaped like an elongated cube, resembled the actual washboats that could be seen along the Seine at the time. But it could also be a name given in jest, since the building had only one supply of water for dozens of apartments.

BOTH REAL AND FAKE WINDMILLS

There have been some 15 windmills in Montmartre, because the hilltop is particularly well exposed to the wind. Only two remain: the Blute-Fin and the Radet, which were transformed into a ballroom in the 19th century called the **Moulin de la Galette**. The Radet has since been moved to the intersection of Rue Girardon and Rue Lepic, and now houses a restaurant. As for the **Moulin Rouge**, its windmill is fake, but acts as a genuine sign for an entertainment venue created in 1889.

A RABBIT IN A SAUCEPAN

When the painter André Gil was commissioned to create the sign for the Cabaret des Assassins, a meeting place for songwriters and poets, he painted a rabbit in a suit escaping from a pot. The cabaret of "Gil's rabbit" (Lapin à Gil) became **Au Lapin Agile**, the new name of the establishment.

THE DONKEY THAT PAINTED WITH ITS TAIL

In 1910, to mock abstract art, the writer **Roland Dorgelès** tied a paintbrush to the tail of the donkey Lolo, who belonged to the owner of Le Lapin Agile. The smeared canvas was exhibited at an official exhibition and met with great success... until the trick was revealed!

WHITER THAN WHITE

The limestone used to build the **Sacré-Coeur** has the double advantage of being hard and self-cleaning in the rain. It comes from the Château-Landon quarries, just south of Paris, which were also used to build the Arc de Triomphe.

Bateau-Lavoir
13 Place Émile-Goudeau
75018 Paris

Au Lapin Agile
22 Rue des Saules
75018 Paris
01 46 06 85 87
au-lapin-agile.com

Moulin de la Galette
3 Avenue Junot
75018 Paris
moulindelagaletteparis.com
01 46 06 84 77

ORSAY, THE STATION THAT BECAME A MUSEUM

It has a large clock on its facade, statues depicting southwestern French towns, and a high glass roof: before it was a museum, Orsay was a railway station. Inaugurated in 1900 as the "Gare d'Orléans," it proved impractical and by 1939 trains no longer ran through the station. Fallen into disuse, it was repurposed several times before being completely refurbished and turned into a museum by the architect Gae Aulenti, to exhibit art from the second half of the 19th century, starting with the Impressionist collections.

The Gare d'Orsay at the beginning of the 20th century

The museum's main hall

GIANT BEASTS

A bronze horse, elephant and rhinoceros have pride of place in the museum's main hall. These imposing statues come from the Trocadero gardens, designed alongside the palace with the same name for the 1878 Universal Exhibition. Inside the museum, you'll find other famous animal sculptures, such as François Pompon's **White Bear**, in the large central aisle.

IMPRESSION, IMPRESSIONNISTS...

Claude Monet, Edgar Degas, Paul Cézanne, Auguste Renoir: the works of these young painters were rejected by the official art salons, so in 1874, they organized their own exhibition of their paintings. When referring to the painting *Impression, Sunrise** by Monet, a journalist invented the word "**impressionist**" to make fun of the painter... without realizing he had just named the art movement destined to become the most famous in the world.

*A painting which is not at the Musée d'Orsay but at the Musée Marmottan (2 Place Louis-Bailly 75016 Paris).

Impression, Sunrise, by Claude Monet

FUNNY WAYS (OF PAINTING)

For the Impressionists, the most important thing was not the subject but the feeling of the moment. They usually painted outdoors—not in studios—to better capture the atmosphere of a place. Even if it meant painting Rouen Cathedral five times (as Monet did), with different colored strokes depending on the **changing light**. This was new... and is still largely misunderstood by the public, who prefer the precise contours of classical painters.

LIFE, PUT SIMPLY

Rather than historical or mythological scenes, which were very popular at the time, the Impressionists wanted their paintings to reflect their era: that of the railway stations and **modern Paris** that had just been built by Haussmann. While they appreciated scenes of daily life, they were also very fond of **landscapes around the capital** or on the Normandy coast, which enabled them to capture the changing effects of the sun and shadows on a stretch of water or a field.

The Canal Saint-Martin, by Alfred Sisley

Still Life with Apples and Oranges, by Paul Cézanne

Dance at Le Moulin de la Galette, by Auguste Renoir

THESE IMPRESSIONNISTS ARE BLURRY!

The Impressionists painted without any preliminary drawings, using small, rapid brushstrokes applied next to each other. Colors were decomposed (orange was obtained by juxtaposing yellow and red) and their layering created the impression of volume that made shapes vibrate, such as in Claude Monet's ***Water Lilies***.

MODERN ARCHITECTURE: YOU WON'T BELIEVE YOUR EYES!

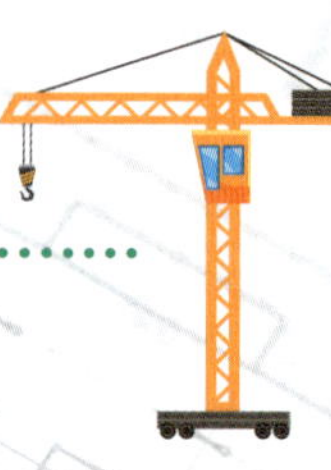

Building never stops in Paris: housing, but also museums, administrative buildings and cultural centers. Some of them are worth taking a look at...

"THE NOTRE-DAME OF PIPES"

When they built the **Pompidou Center** (also known as Beaubourg) in 1977, the architects Piano and Rogers put everything that's usually hidden at the front and painted it in bright colors: electrical fittings in yellow, water pipes in green and ventilation in blue. Everything that goes up and down—escalators and elevators—is marked in bright red. The nickname "Notre-Dame de la Tuyauterie" (Our Lady of Pipes) given to the building at the time of its inauguration shows just how little people thought of this place, which is now so widely appreciated by everyone.

A GIANT PÉTANQUE BALL

Beneath its dome made of 6,433 steel triangles, the **Géode** has housed a cinema since 1985 with an 85-foot-diameter semi-spherical screen, one of the largest in the world. Films in Imax are projected at 180 degrees, like a life-size sound and light show. It's fabulous for discovering the mysteries of space and sea monsters!

THE GREEN WALL OF AN ASTONISHING MUSEUM

It's rare for a gardener to decorate walls. Except at the **Musée du Quai Branly-Jacques-Chirac**, dedicated to primitive arts (the artistic production of indigenous civilizations), where in 2004 Patrick Blanc covered an 8,610-square-foot wall with 15,000 plants of 150 different species. Attached to felt panels, they are supplied with water from the roof via an invisible network of sprinklers.

A GREEN SNAKE

It appeared in 2008 on the Quai d'Austerlitz: the metal structure of the **Cité de la Mode et du Design** features a grand staircase serving the Institut Français de la Mode, the Musée d'Art Ludique, restaurants and, at the top, a terrace that transforms into a nightclub in the summer.

A STRANGE SAILBOAT!

A ship with 12 sails billowing in the wind? Or a complex construction of glass and concrete forming walls, roofs and terraces? Designed by architect Frank Gehry in 2014, the **Fondation Louis-Vuitton** is as modern and astonishing as the works it exhibits.

THE PARIS PHILHARMONIC SPREADS ITS WINGS

This concert hall with 2,400 seats, designed by the architect **Jean Nouvel**, opened in 2015. Its facade and roof are covered with 265,000 aluminium birds.

Pompidou Center
Place Georges-Pompidou
75004 Paris
01 44 78 12 33
centrepompidou.fr

La Géode
26 Avenue Corentin-Cariou
75019 Paris
01 40 05 79 99
lageode.fr

Musée du Quai-Branly-Jacques-Chirac
37 Quai Branly
75007 Paris
01 56 61 70 00
quaibranly.fr

Cité de la Mode et du Design
34 Quai d'Austerlitz
75013 Paris
01 76 77 25 30
citemodedesign.fr

Fondation Louis-Vuitton
8 Avenue du Mahatma-Gandhi
75116 Paris
01 40 69 96 00
fondationlouisvuitton.fr

Philharmonie de Paris
221 Avenue Jean-Jaurès
75019 Paris
01 44 84 44 84
philharmoniedeparis.fr

STATUES THAT TELL A STORY

The main squares in Paris are adorned with a monumental statue in the middle. The king, liberty, victory, the great figures of France: their theme is often linked to history. There's a statue for every square!

NOTHING BUT TWISTS AND TURNS!
NAPOLEON I, PLACE VENDÔME

Perched high above the ground, he's hard to see. Dressed in Roman style, like Julius Caesar, it is indeed Napoleon who stands on top of the column built in 1810 to celebrate his **military victories**. Although he seems out of reach, the Emperor has been lowered from his perch several times... before being hoisted up again. The first statue of Napoleon in a toga was removed and melted down in 1814, before a new one replaced it in 1833, this time with Napoleon dressed as a corporal. 30 years later, Napoleon III had the second statue replaced by a third one, again in Roman style. During the Paris Commune, the column was pulled down... and the statue with it. It had to be restored before it could return to its original position in 1875. And stay there.

A PIECE OF EGYPT!
THE VICTORY, PLACE DU CHÂTELET

The palm tree sculpted at the base of the column and the four sphinxes surrounding the fountain commemorate France's victories in Egypt. It was **General Bonaparte** who decided to build the monument on the site of the great Châtelet, a fortress demolished in 1802.

At the bottom of the column on Place du Châtelet, four sphinxes are watching you...

JUST SO YOU KNOW, THERE'S ONLY ONE GENIUS HERE...

COME ON CHILDREN... CALM DOWN!

IT SHINES BRIGHTLY!
THE GENIUS OF LIBERTY, PLACE DE LA BASTILLE

This golden, winged genie brandishing the broken chains of tyranny does not celebrate the storming of the Bastille fortress on July 14, 1789. Rather, it pays homage to the **July 1830 Revolution**, during which Parisians overthrew King Charles X. Beneath the column's vast circular base lie the remains of the 504 victims claimed by the uprising, whose names are engraved all along the column. After the revolution, King Louis-Philippe came to power. When, in 1848, he was ousted by a new revolution, his throne was burnt at the foot of the July Column, and those who died in the barricades were buried alongside the previous graves.

A MAJOR SYMBOL!
MARIANNE, PLACE DE LA RÉPUBLIQUE

Standing at nearly 33 feet high, Marianne, the symbol of the French Republic, brandishes an olive branch in her right hand and holds the table of human rights with her left. She has stood at the center of the square since 1883, while at her feet stand the three statues of Liberty, Equality and Fraternity, illustrating the **Republican motto**.

La Liberté, l'Égalité et la Fraternité, Marianne's maids of honor

THE SEINE: A BUSTLING RIVER

The river has always been part of Parisians' history. Until the 1930s, people swam in it. This experience is not recommended nowadays and is even forbidden, since the water is not very clean and there is heavy boat traffic.

EVERYBODY TO SHELTER, ZOUAVE IS TAKING A DIP!

The water level of the Seine varies between 11.2 and 18.7 feet high. To find out if the water is rising, a good indicator is the **Zouave statue on the Pont de l'Alma**, which is 16 feet high: when its feet are in the water, that means the river is rising. In June 2016, the water rose to 20 feet: up to Zouave's thighs!

Zouave on Pont de l'Alma

WHAT A CATASTROPHE!

In **January 1910**, Zouave had water up to his neck. The Seine had risen to over 26 feet, having broken its banks and flooded the roads, cellars and the metro. 20,000 buildings were damaged and people had to navigate the roads in boats or on wooden planks. It was the biggest rise in the water's level since 1658.

LET THE FIGURES SAIL BY!

In Paris, the Seine stretches over 8 miles

The average temperature of the water is 57°F

37 bridges cross the river, whose current runs at around 1.25 miles per hour

OOH! OOH! I THINK IT'S A BIG ONE!

THEY'RE BITING!

No longer as polluted as it was in the 1970s, the Seine has rewelcomed its fish population. **Carp, trout, perch and pike** await amateur fishermen, often stationed around the Île Saint-Louis or Île de la Cité. However, as the fish are contaminated with heavy metals, it is forbidden to eat them...

BATEAU-MOUCHE, WHAT A FUNNY NAME!

The **tourist boats** sailing down the Seine are called "bateau-mouche", or "fly boats". This is not because they resemble flies, however, but because the first ones to be made–in 1867–came from the Mouche district in Lyon.

BOATS ON THE WATER

With an 11-mile-per-hour speed limit, the use of sails forbidden and strict traffic rules to follow, boating down the Seine is not something to be done without prior preparation! To monitor the traffic, a **river brigade** has been carrying out surveillance of the river since 1900.

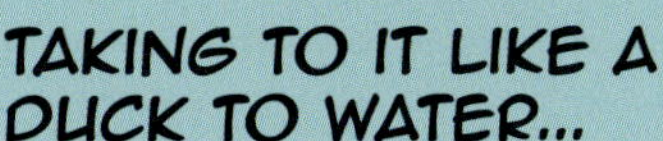

TAKING TO IT LIKE A DUCK TO WATER...

Just like the floating baths from the 17th century, the **Joséphine Baker swimming pool** is attached to the edge of the Seine and has been open since 2006. With its removable roof and unrivaled view of the river, it's the best place to take a dip.

Piscine Joséphine-Baker
Quai François-Mauriac
75013 Paris
01 56 61 96 50
piscine-baker.fr

ALONG THE CANALS

The canals were created in the early 19th century to supply Paris with water and transport goods by avoiding having to turn along the Seine. The longest one is the Canal de l'Ourcq, which collects water 60 miles from Paris and carries it to the Bassin de la Villette. From here, the Canal Saint-Martin—the shortest one—ends at the Bassin de l'Arsenal. The Canal Saint-Denis links the Canal de l'Ourcq, near the Parc de la Villette, to the Seine, 3 miles north of Paris.

LOCKS, A USER'S GUIDE

To be navigable, a canal has to deal with the difference in height between different locations. For the Canal Saint-Martin, the difference is 82 feet between the Bassin de la Villette and the Seine. Quite a climb! And boats can't go up stairs... So what's the solution? The **locks** form a chamber in which the water level can be varied, so that the boat can "go up" or "go down" by several feet and continue on its way.

QUITE SOME TRAFFIC!

The Canal Saint-Martin can be used by 385-ton **barges**, although today it's mainly used by pleasure boats. The Canal Saint-Denis, on the other hand, can accommodate barges of up to 1,100 tons! These huge boats mainly transport construction materials and sand or gravel used on Parisian building sites, or remove rubble from demolition sites.

SAD FISHING HAUL...

The Canal Saint-Martin regularly undergoes a thorough cleaning.

Beneath the mud that's removed, you'll always find incredible trash: bicycles, shopping carts, motorcycles, scooters, armchairs, construction site barriers, bed frames, bottles, kitchen utensils and even... a toilet!

MY CANAL IS NOT A TRASH CAN!

BRIDGES OF ALL KINDS

To cross the canals, there are several solutions: there are narrow, high footbridges reserved for pedestrians, raised static bridges—to allow barges and their cargo to pass through—and swing bridges, such as the **Grange-aux-Belles** bridge on the Canal Saint-Martin. It is unique in the way it opens by swinging to the side when a boat approaches.

THE CANAL UNDER THE SIDEWALK...

Underneath the cobblestones on Place de la Bastille is where the Canal Saint-Martin flows! It is **buried** beneath the boulevards Richard-Lenoir and Jules-Ferry and emerges into the open air at the Port de l'Arsenal. 1.25 miles underground, dimly lit by giant eye-shaped openings is Europe's longest stone vault.

From street level, it's hard to imagine you're walking over the canal!

CRUISES, PÉTANQUE AND PICNICS

For several years now, the canals have been open spaces for leisure activities. You can stroll along their banks, play pétanque, have a picnic or listen to music. From the Port de l'Arsenal, **mini-cruises** take you several miles up the Canal Saint-Martin to the Bassin de la Villette.

UNDER THE BRIDGES

No fewer than 37 bridges line the eight miles of the Seine's course through Paris, but, for a long time—until almost the middle of the Middle Ages—there were only three, each crossing an arm of the river on either side of the Île de la Cité.

THE FIRST ONES

In ancient times, the Romans built the **Petit-Pont** linking the left bank to the Île de la Cité, and the **Grand-Pont** between the Île de la Cité and the right bank. This extended the *cardo*, the main street running from south to north through Lutèce, towards the river. Of course, these two bridges have been rebuilt several times since antiquity. The Petit-Pont is now called Petit-Pont-Cardinal-Lustiger, and the Grand-Pont, Pont Notre-Dame.

THE OLDEST ONE

Despite its name, the **Pont-Neuf** ("New Bridge") is the oldest surviving bridge in Paris. Completed in 1607, it was the first to cross the Seine at its widest point, and the first not to have a row of houses on either side; Parisians could now enjoy a view of the river. It was King Henri IV who commissioned its construction, and whose equestrian statue adorns the central platform.

THE MOST METALLIC ONE

Thanks Napoleon! In 1801, he ordered the construction of the **Pont des Arts**, Paris' first metal footbridge. It was rebuilt in 1984 after its partial collapse, and today is a popular spot for walkers, lovers and picnickers.

Pont des Arts

Petit-Pont

Pont-Neuf

SO, ARE WE JUMPING IN?

YOU GO FIRST! I'LL WATCH YOU...

1. Pont amont
2. Pont National
3. Pont de Tolbiac
4. Passerelle Simone-de-Beauvoir
5. Pont de Bercy
6. Pont Charles-de-Gaulle
7. Viaduc d'Austerlitz
8. Pont d'Austerlitz
9. Pont de Sully
10. Pont de la Tournelle
11. Pont Marie
12. Pont Louis-Philippe
13. Pont Saint-Louis
14. Pont de l'Archevêché
15. Pont au Double
16. Pont d'Arcole
17. Petit-Pont
18. Pont Notre-Dame
19. Pont Saint-Michel
20. Pont au Change
21. Pont-Neuf
22. Pont des Arts
23. Pont du Carrousel
24. Pont Royal
25. Passerelle Léopold-Sédar-Senghor
26. Pont de la Concorde
27. Pont Alexandre-III
28. Pont des Invalides
29. Pont de l'Alma
30. Passerelle Debilly
31. Pont d'Iéna
32. Pont de Bir-Hakeim
33. Pont Rouelle
34. Pont de Grenelle
35. Pont Mirabeau
36. Pont du Garigliano
37. Pont aval

The 37 bridges of Paris (from upstream to downstream)

THE MOST RUSSIAN ONE

Inaugurated during the 1900 Universal Exhibition the **Pont Alexandre-III**, named after the tsar, celebrates the friendship between France and Russia. Four columns topped with winged and gilded statues frame its entrance.

THE BEST-LIT ONE

This is the **Pont du Carrousel**, linking the Quai des Tuileries to the Quai Voltaire. When it was rebuilt in 1935, it featured a spectacular innovation: telescopic lampposts. Standing at 40 feet high during the day, so as not to obstruct the view of the Louvre, they rise to 62 feet at night to cast their light far and wide.

THE MOST RECENT ONE

The latest addition to the Parisian bridge family, the **Passerelle Simone-de-Beauvoir** was built in 2006, and bears the name of a famous 20th-century writer. Its two steel curves intertwine between the François-Mitterrand library and the Parc de Bercy, and it is reserved for cyclists and pedestrians.

Pont Alexandre-III

Passerelle Simone-de-Beauvoir

Pont du Carrousel

SECRETS OF THE METRO

Just below street level or sometimes buried deeper, the metro lines weave their way through Paris. And they cross the Seine thanks to watertight containers which were assembled above ground and then submerged beneath the riverbed. The Paris metro transports over five million people every day.

PARIS WAS A BIT BEHIND...

The **first metro** was built in London in 1863, followed by New York in 1868. Paris didn't take the initiative until 1898, so that the city would have its own metro by the time the Universal Exhibition opened its doors in April 1900. It was a bit of a failure, as line 1 was not opened until July 19. This first line linked Porte Maillot to Porte de Vincennes with three-car trains... serving just eight stations. The remaining ten would come into service in September 1900.

BRAVO MONSIEUR BIENVENÜE!

Heading a team of 2,000 people, the engineer **Fulgence Bienvenüe** drew up the metro plan, directed the construction site and organized the network. It was initially conceived as a large cross on the map of Paris, with an east-west axis (line 1) a north-south axis (line 4) and a large loop running from Place de l'Étoile to Nation (line 2), then from Nation to Étoile via the left bank (line 6). By the time Bienvenüe retired in 1932, 14 lines were in operation. Today, the engineer's name is associated with Montparnasse station.

A DENSE NETWORK!

Wherever you are in Paris, there's always a metro station 550 yards away at most. With its **303 stations**, it's the densest subway network in Europe.

Concorde Station

THE HIGHS AND LOWS OF THE METRO

The longest is **line 13**, which runs from Châtillon-Montrouge to Asnières-Genevilliers/Saint-Denis, covering 15 miles. In contrast, **line 3 bis**, which runs from Gambetta station to Porte-des-Lilas station and measures 0.8 miles, is the shortest in the Paris network. The speed record is held by Meteor, the automatic, unmanned **line 14**, which travels at 25 miles per hour from Mairie de Saint-Ouen to Olympiades. Running twice as slow, **line 4** (Porte-de-Clignancourt to Bagneux-Lucie Aubrac) travels at just 12 miles per hour. **Line 1**, which is used by over 720,000 passengers a day, is the busiest. It runs from Château-de-Vincennes to La Défense.

FAMOUS STATIONS...

• **Concorde, the most democratic**
On the ceramic-tiled walls is the text from the 1789 Declaration of Human Rights, with no spaces or punctuation between the words.

• **Abbesses, the deepest**
Perched on Montmartre hill, this station is 98 feet underground. Fortunately, an elevator brings passengers up to street level.

• **Arts-et-Métiers, the most futuristic**
With its copper plating and gold nuts and bolts, it feels like stepping inside the *Nautilus*, the sub-marine described in Jules Verne's novel *Twenty Thousand Leagues Under the Sea*. It's a scientific taster of what's on offer at the Musée des Arts et Métiers close by.

GHOSTS OF THE METRO

Some stations, which were closed during the Second World War or abandoned just after being built, are real ghost stations, which never see trains of passengers pass through. An example is one of the platforms at the Porte-des-Lilas station which is reserved for film shoots.

SEVEN STATIONS FOR MILLIONS OF TRAVELERS

Paris has seven passenger stations in operation: Saint-Lazare, Nord, Est, Lyon, Montparnasse, Bercy and Austerlitz. The first stations, which are veritable historical monuments, were built in the mid-19th century, as soon as railroad lines were introduced. These stations serve the whole of France, welcoming hundreds of thousands of passengers every day.

La gare Saint-Lazare, Claude Monet, 1877

THE IMPRESSIONNISTS' STATION

When it was built in 1837, the **Gare Saint-Lazare** (the oldest railway station in Paris) was a simple wooden passenger platform on the first railroad line from Paris to Saint-Germain. Transformed and enlarged in the years that followed, it inspired Impressionist painters, notably Claude Monet, who painted it a dozen times.

CAN YOU HEAR SIMONE?

In every station across Paris and the rest of France, it's always the same voice! It's Simone Hérault, the "voice of the SNCF." For over 30 years, this former radio presenter with her soothing voice has announced all the messages informing passengers about trains and station activities, either in full sentences or in words that are recorded, stored and digitally assembled.

THE MOST FREQUENTED STATION IN EUROPE!

Gare du Nord, opened in 1846, links up with all of northern France, Belgium, Germany, the Netherlands and London since the Eurostar service started: it is the most frequented in Europe, with almost 200 million travelers a year passing through. On the station's facade statues represent the main cities of the "Paris Nord" line. The current station was rebuilt in 1866 by Jacques Hittorff, while the former facade was reinstated... in Lille: it's on the current Lille-Flandres station building.

Gare du Nord

Gare Montparnasse, October 22, 1895

AN ACCIDENT THAT MADE SOME NOISE!

On October 22, 1895, the steam locomotive on the Granville-Paris train failed to brake on arrival at **Gare Montparnasse**. It ploughed through the concourse, ripped open the facade and ended up with its nose on the square outside. The accident claimed just one victim, an unfortunate newsagent standing just below.

The Ruisseau Gardens

TAKE A STROLL ALONG THE TRACKS

All around Paris, on the route of the former **Petite Ceinture** line, which was in operation until 1934, platforms at disused stations have been transformed into shared gardens. Ornano station, for example, has become the Ruisseau Gardens.

Jardins du Ruisseau
110 bis, rue du Ruisseau
75018 Paris
06 51 25 16 23
lesjardinsduruisseau.fr

MINI TRAINS FOR BIG FANS

Hiding beneath the tracks at **Gare de l'Est** are the small premises of AFAC, the Association des Amis du Chemin de Fer. A miniature rail network stretches across 656 yards, with around 100 switches, traffic lights, stations and trains hurtling along at 4 mph. Controlling the circuits are serious rail enthusiasts who share their passion for model trains with the public every Saturday.

Mini trains at Gare de l'Est

AFAC, Association des Amis du Chemin de Fer
Gare de l'Est
75010 Paris
01 40 38 20 92
afac.asso.fr

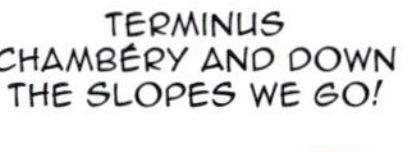

FUNNY PARKS

Paris has over 400 parks, gardens and squares, not including the Bois de Boulogne and the Bois de Vincennes. But in Europe's most densely populated capital, you need some imagination to grow even a blade of grass.

FOLIES IN THE MEADOW

The **Parc de la Villette** is the "green lung" of Paris. Created in 1979 by Bernard Tschumi on the site of a former slaughterhouse, it alternates dedicated play areas, like the Jardin d'Éole, with bright red structures called "folies" and fields for relaxing or having a picnic.

IN THE JUNGLE OF BOOKS

The garden at the **François-Mitterrand Library** is a mini underground forest which although inaccessible to the public, can be appreciated from the reading rooms.

PERCHED UP ON A STATION

The **Jardin Atlantique**, which you can't see from the street, is planted above the railway and on top of the Gare Montparnasse parking lot.

SHALL WE GET CHICKEN AND CHIPS AFTERWARDS?

HEY! GIVE US A SMILE!

JUST LIKE IN THE MOUNTAINS

The **Alpine Garden**, in the Jardin des Plantes, is dug out ten feet below soil level to create slopes and contours, because mountain plants are grown here, in a setting that resembles their native environment as closely as possible.

WITH AN INCREDIBLE VIEW

The **Coulée Verte**, which is planted with trees and flowers, stands at 23 feet high and zigzags three miles across the city, from the Viaduct des Arts, near the Bastille Opera House, up to the city ring road.

THE FUNNIEST ONE

On a 30-degree slope at the **Parc de Belleville** you'll find the most original play area, with a giant hut, a ship, and a dinosaur to climb up and then slide down.

BUILDINGS AND HOUSES

While light-colored stone buildings, with their large windows and balconies, embody the typical Parisian dwelling, this is not the only style. And almost every street in Paris has its own surprises in store for those who enjoy observing its facades.

BRICK AND STONE FOR HENRI IV

On the Île de la Cité, **Place Dauphine** was created by Henri IV in 1607. Its brick-and-stone houses had archways on the ground floor; over time they have been remodeled but the two buildings that look out onto the Pont-Neuf have remained the same.
On the Left Bank, Rue Dauphine has also retained some of its 17th-century buildings. **Place des Vosges**, whose construction began a few years earlier in the Marais, has two floors of apartments with slate roofs and small-paned windows.

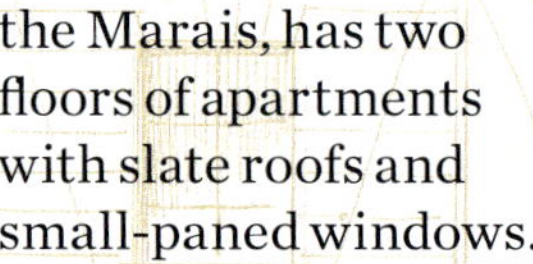

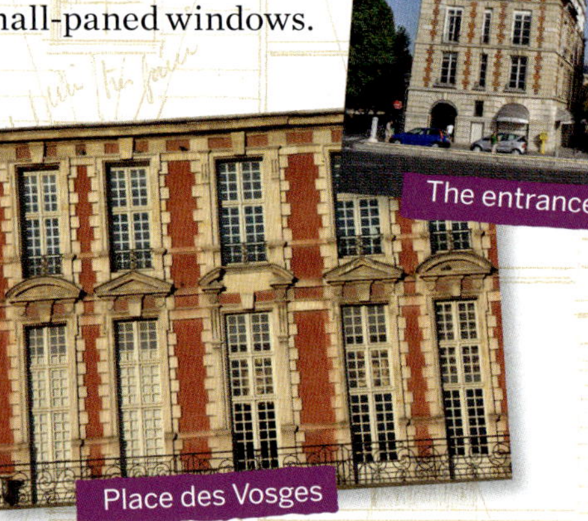

The entrance to Place Dauphine

Place des Vosges

THE OLDEST HOUSE IN PARIS

Located at 51 Rue de Montmorency, it belonged to **Nicolas Flamel**, who had it built in 1407 to house the poor. The owner's intials, as well as the building's date, are engraved on the facade of this four-story building which has three doors.

VERY SPECIAL MANSIONS

Of the 2,000 private mansions which have existed in Paris at one point or another, only 400 remain. These are stone residences with huge reception rooms which housed rich, noble or upper-class families. With gardens and courtyard entrances, these mansions have often been transformed into embassies, government ministries or even city halls, like the one in the 9th arrondissement, the former **Hôtel d'Augny**.

THE BARON WHO CHANGED PARIS

With light-colored stone, large windows and balconies on the third and sixth floors... many Parisian buildings are based on the model designed in the 19th century by Prefect **Georges Eugène Haussmann**. Appointed in 1853 by Napoleon III, he transformed the capital into a vast construction site. What resulted were wide, tree-lined avenues, parks and squares, and thousands of brand-new buildings in an elegant, functional style dubbed... Haussmannian.

NICE APARTMENTS AT AFFORDABLE PRICES

Recognizable by their high brick facades, these low-cost housing units (called **HBM**) were built after the First World War alongside the former fortifications around Paris. Designed for low-income families, with running water and gas lighting, they are more elegant than the concrete HLMs built in the 1970s.

A DOLL'S HOUSE

At 39 Rue du Château-d'Eau is the smallest house in Paris, which is four feet wide and has only one story.

LONG LIVE GREEN SPACES!

At 17-19 Rue des Orteaux, in the 20th arrondissement, the building has gone eco-friendly. There are solar panels, green roofs, geothermal heating, rain-water barrels and a central garden, all of which turned an unsanitary space into a lovely place to live which is 100% natural!

THOUSANDS OF STREETS

From private passageways to big boulevards, from the center of town to the Bois de Boulogne and Bois de Vincennes, the capital is criss-crossed by more than 6,300 roads. Put end to end, they would form a 1056-mile-long strip, not including the 22-mile ring road. Since the 18th century, their names have appeared on plaques affixed to the first and last houses on every street, as well as at every intersection.

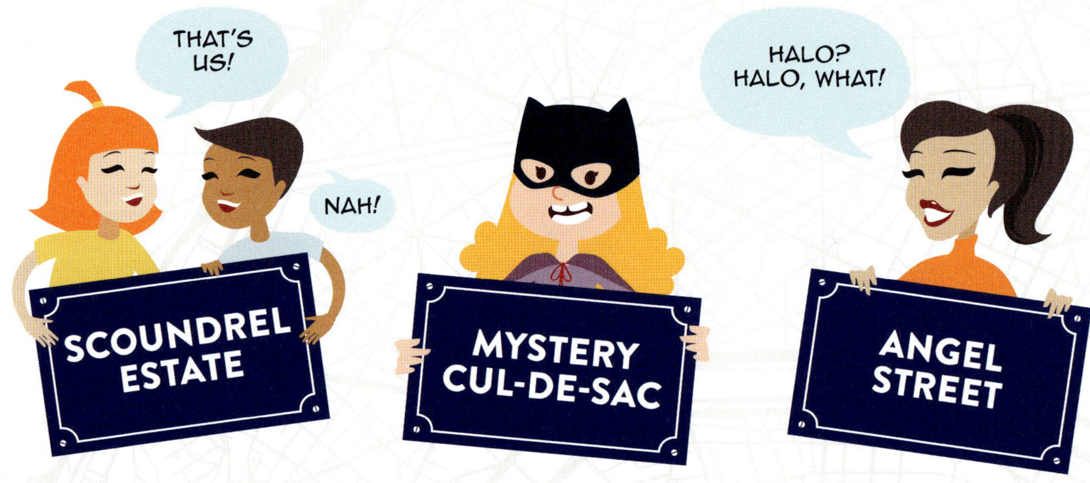

WHO NAMES THE STREETS?

Beautiful avenues, shopping streets or pedestrianized precincts, they all have a name to help you find your way around. The privilege of naming them falls to the **city council**. But any citizen can put forward suggestions relating to particular events or famous residents, who must have been dead for at least five years.

IT'S EASY TO WORK OUT WHERE YOU ARE...

Since 1805, thanks to a system invented under Napoleon by Prefect Nicolas Frochot, the **Seine has served as a landmark**. Streets running parallel to it are numbered in the direction of the river's current, from east to west. Perpendicular streets are numbered from the Seine towards the suburbs at the city gates. Even numbers are always on the right and odd numbers are on the left.

While the street signs are (almost always) identical, the numbers on the buildings are a bit more whimsical.

...BUT THERE ARE EXCEPTIONS!

Several streets in the 12th arrondissement don't follow the rule: despite being parallel to the Seine, they are numbered in the **opposite direction of the river's current**. This is the case for Avenue Daumesnil, Rues de Reuilly, de Wattignies, Rue de Charenton and also Rue de Picpus.

NICE CLEAN STREETS

The 1,056 miles of streets are vacuumed and washed at least once a week by staff from the Service Technique de la Propreté de Paris.

Heavily-used thoroughfares (the ring road, expressways and underground roads, etc.) are cleaned at night, in sections, to minimize disruption to traffic.

THE MINI STREET WHERE NOBODY LIVES

Rue des Degrés, between Rues de Cléry and Beauregard, in the Bonne-Nouvelle district, is the shortest road in Paris measuring just under 19 feet. Another special feature is that it's made up of a 14-step staircase–which explains its name–and it doesn't lead to any dwelling.

THE NARROWEST STREET...

Officially, it's the Rue du Chat-qui-Pêche in the Latin Quarter, named after an old business there, measuring 5.9 feet wide. However **Sentier des Merisiers**, in the 12th arrondissement, narrows down to 34 inches in some places!

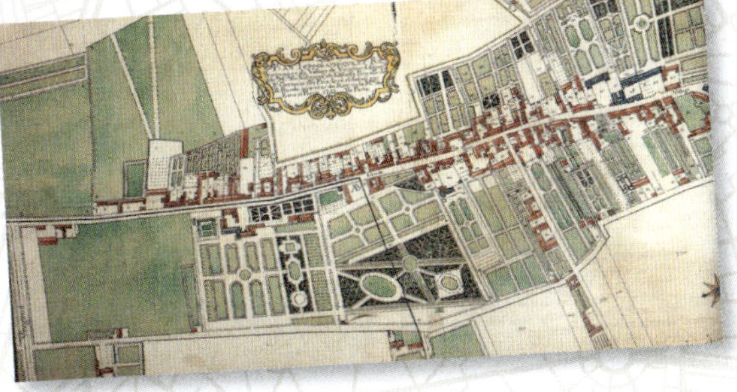

... AND THE LONGEST

Straddling the 6th and 15th arrondissements, **Rue de Vaugirard** is 2.7 miles long and has 407 house numbers. The road used to lead to the former Vaugirard village, which joined Paris in 1860.

HELP!

What's the scariest street in Paris? Is it the Rue Vide-Gousset, whose name recalls the pockets (or gussets) swiftly robbed by thieves? Or is it Rue de la Petite Truanderie, Rue de la Grande-Truanderie or Rue des Mauvais-Garçons? Dark and notorious, they were once real cut-throat areas and were named accordingly.

SECRETS OF THE PASSAGES

Either carved out between buildings or built at the same time as them, the covered passages created in the first half of the 19th century were the forerunners of shopping malls. Thanks to their glass roofs, they enabled passers-by to window-shop without being exposed to the elements.

FOR TAKING SHELTER IN THE HEART OF THE CITY

Located on the Right Bank, the covered passages are mainly concentrated between the Grands Boulevards and the Palais-Royal. Many have disappeared, but around 20 have survived in Paris.

Passage des Panoramas

BEAUTY CONTEST

Galerie Vivienne, with its mosaic floors and elegant boutiques, is usually top of the list for strollers who appreciate its chic atmosphere. But you might prefer **Passage Jouffroy**, the first to feature a metal roof structure and even underfloor heating, **Passage des Panoramas** with its period lighting fixtures, or the charming **Galerie Véro-Dodat**.

Galerie Vivienne

Galerie Véro-Dodat

TEMPTATIONS BY THE HUNDREDS

In the passages, you can find cafés, restaurants and tea rooms, boutiques selling clothes, toys and collector items, bookstores, beautiful stationery... And in Passage Jouffroy, you can even see the Musée Grévin's waxworks in the window displays.

Galerie du Palais-Royal

Passage Jouffroy

TREASURES UNDER THE ARCADES

The open-air but sheltered **galleries of the Palais-Royal** also attract strollers. Under their arcades are picturesque boutiques, such as those dedicated to toy soldiers, medals and flags in the Galerie de Chartres.

COME ON MADAME, HURRY ALONG! WE HAVE AN APPOINTMENT AT THE SHOE-CLEANING SALON!

CLEANLINESS GUARANTEED!

Set back from the dirtiness of the streets, the passages—at least the more chic ones—were true salons where high society met, shopped and chatted. At the entrance, clothes and shoes were cleaned in **scrubbing rooms** and, for a more complete treatment, luxurious public baths compensated for the absence of bathtubs in people's apartments.

PARIS-BOMBAY

Less luxurious than the other Parisian passages, **Passage Brady**, near Porte Saint-Denis, is by the far the most picturesque: nicknamed “Little India,” it houses many Indian restaurants, barber shops, spice sellers and vendors of multicolored saris...

Passage Brady

GHOSTS, HIDDEN TREASURE, LEGENDS AND MIRACLES

Paris isn't lacking intriguing stories... both real and imaginary. They are an alternative way to discover the capital...

Nicolas Flamel

HE WALKED WITH HIS HEAD CUT OFF...

Around the year 250, **the bishop of Paris, Denis,** was beheaded by the Romans along with his two companions, Eleuthère and Rustique. The hill where they were executed became known as *mons martyrium* ("mount of martyrs" in Latin), which later became Montmartre. But the most extraordinary fact is that, after his execution, Denis is said to have picked up his head and started walking north, collapsing a few miles further on... where the basilica of Saint-Denis would later be erected in the town of the same name.

THE ALCHEMIST

Nicolas Flamel was a scribe and bookseller. He married a wealthy woman in 1370 and set about helping the poor by building several houses for them. But it was not so much his generosity that made him famous as the legend claiming that he had found, in an old book, the means to transform ordinary metals into gold, and even the secret to eternal life! Many swore, long after the Middle Ages, that they had come across this genius alchemist in the streets of Paris.

A MAGICIAN WHO GRANTS WISHES

To have your wishes granted, all you have to do is stand in front of **Allan Kardec**'s tombstone in the Père-Lachaise cemetery. At least, this what the man's followers believed: in the mid-19th century, Allan Kardec pioneered the art of spiritism, i.e. the art of making tables turn and spirits talk.

Allan Kardec's tomb

The Phantom of the Opera, adapted for the American movies from 1925.

THE PHANTOM OF THE OPERA

In **Gaston Leroux**'s novel, published in 1910, this phantom lives in the basements of the Palais Garnier, near a large water tank. He is supposedly a pianist who was disfigured in the fire at the former opera house on Rue Le Peletier and is said to have sought refuge in the new opera house during its construction. In reality, a skeleton was indeed discovered in the Opéra Garnier's cellar, but it belonged to a rebel from the Paris Commune and not a ghost-pianist!

THE CURSE OF THE KNIGHTS TEMPLAR

In the Middle Ages, the Knights Templar were a prosperous and powerful military and religious order. In Paris, they owned and controlled a fortress and a district (around today's Rue du Temple). During the Crusades, they were even responsible for guarding the royal treasury. This power eventually irritated King Philip the Fair. He dissolved the order and had the brotherhood's leader, **Jacques de Molay**, burned alive in 1314 on a small island on the site of today's Square du Vert-Galant. While dying in the flames, the Grand Master of the Knights Templar put a curse on Philip the Fair and his descendants. All would later perish, either violently or prematurely. Was it a curse or pure chance?

GAROU-GAROU, THE WALL-CROSSER

Garou-Garou, a character invented by writer Marcel Aymé, has the power to walk through walls. Handy for launching a career as a burglar or escaping from prison! Until one day, he found himself trapped in a wall on Rue Norvins in Montmartre... where his statue can still be admired.

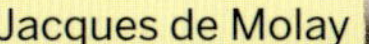

Jacques de Molay

PRETTY SIGNS

In days gone by, every shop had its own sign. Made of wood or brightly painted metal sheeting, they indicated the store's speciality in words and, for the many people who couldn't read, in images. If you look up, you'll still see a few in Paris, particularly in the Les Halles district.

BEAUTIFUL BEES

On the **corner of Rues Rambuteau and Pierre-Lescot**, four bees pose on a hive covered in straw to point out a honey merchant's store, which no longer exists.

LE ROCHER DE CANCALE... IN PARIS

A black rock for a sign, with mussels and clams hanging from it—now that's something! Just as impressive is the beautifully sculpted facade of this restaurant at **78 Rue Montorgueil**. Founded in the early 19th century on the other side of the street, it moved to its current address in 1846, and continues to treat Parisians to oysters and other seafood.

A SNAIL ON RUE MONTORGUEIL

A magnificent golden gastropod with its antennas sticking up sits proudly on top of the awning of this restaurant created in 1832 at **38 Rue Montorgueil**. The establishment was frequented by writers (Marcel Proust), actors (Charlie Chaplin) and painters (Picasso).

EXCEPTIONAL SIGNS

The most famous sign is that of the cabaret Le Chat Noir, located in Pigalle.

The oldest sign, which probably belonged to an inn, is found on 42 Rue Galande. It depicts Saint Julien l'Hospitalier helping Jesus cross a river while he was disguised as a leper in order not to be recognized.

THE LES HALLES BELL

This golden bell on **28 Rue Coquillière** is a replica of the one which, in years gone by, announced the end of the Les Halles market at lunchtime. Beggars would then come running to collect the unsold food for free. This tradition could offer an explanation for the origin of the word "clochard" (beggar), since the word for bell is "cloche." Today, it decorates the frontage of a restaurant.

THE MARAIS THERMOMETER

On the black background of this thermometer, which is just as tall as the windows surrounding it, the red figures indicate the temperature in degrees centigrade. The hardware store that this sign belonged to on **36 Rue de Poitou** no longer exists, but the sign remains.

A SIGN WITH A PLAY ON WORDS

Near the Canal Saint-Martin, on **Rue Jean-Poulmarch**, this powerful feline acted as the sign for an inn called Au Lion d'Or which sounds like "Au lit, on dort!" meaning "Off to bed, time to sleep!").

TREES UNLIKE ANY OTHERS

There are a total of 185,000 trees in Paris, found along avenues, and in public parks and cemeteries. And if we were to include those in the Bois de Boulogne and Bois de Vincennes, we'd have to add another 300,000! Some of them are particularly remarkable.

THE OLDEST

This "pseudo-acacia"—also known as a **black locust**—was planted in 1602 by King Henri IV's gardener, Jean Robin, who gave it its French name "robinier." Its seeds came from North America. Slightly leaning but evergreen, it enjoys a peaceful haven in Square René-Viviani, behind the Saint-Julien-le-Pauvre church.

WAOUH!

THE TASTIEST

The **achiote** is a South American shrub grown in the Auteuil greenhouses. The red seeds from its fruit are used to color the rind of mimolette, the Dutch cheese.

CUI

THE SMALLEST

You can find these miniature trees in the **Bonsai garden** at the Parc Floral. Pruned in a Japanese style, they measure between 5 and 24 inches.

THE MOST "HISTORICAL"

The **silver linden tree** on Place de la Bataille-de-Stalingrad was planted on November 4, 1945 to celebrate the Liberation of Paris.

THE BIGGEST

The oldest tree in the Parc Monceau is an **Oriental plane**, planted in 1814. The circumference of its trunk is... 23 feet! That makes it the thickest tree in Paris.

THE TALLEST

The record holder is very disputed! The **common plane tree** on the Île de Bercy in the Bois de Vincennes is almost 148 feet tall, while another of the same species, in the Allée de Longchamp in the Bois de Boulogne, is over 131 feet tall. In Paris itself, a 131-foot-tall plane tree flourishes in the Parc Montsouris.

THE ONE THAT WILL LIVE FOREVER

The **Lebanese cedar** in the Jardin des Plantes was planted in 1734 by Bernard de Jussieu... but it's still in its infancy because these trees can live for 2,500 years!

THE BEST ACCLIMATIZED

Originating from Asia, **bamboo** covers three-quarters of the Jardin d'Agronomie Tropicale, created on the edge of the Bois de Vincennes for the 1907 Colonial Exhibition.

STRANGE ANIMALS...

It's not all sparrows, dogs and pigeons in Paris. Nearly 2,000 species have been recorded here. But where are these strange animals hiding?

THE WILD (BUT NICE) BURGUNDY RABBIT

This **rabbit**, who is too fat for livestock farming, is fed, just like in the past, on grass and grains at the Ferme de Paris, where he lives out his days in peace on the farm, in the company of calves, cows, donkeys, geese, ducks, sows and pigs, all waiting for visits from Parisians.

Ferme de Paris
1 Route du Pesage
75012 Paris
paris.fr/lieux/
la-ferme-de-paris-6597

BEES IN THE CITY

They produce renowned honey, harvested from **600 hives** installed in the Luxembourg Gardens, on the roofs of the Opéra, in the Bois de Boulogne, and in the Parc Georges-Brassens...

Even the roofs of some Parisian buildings are covered with beehives. The capital has the advantage of offering a wide variety of plants and flowers, which are far less contaminated with pesticides than some fields.

FISH FROM THE DEPTHS OF TIME

Lungfish are the last representatives of a species that is... 300 million years old! They are among the 5,000 fish, invertebrates and saurians in the aquarium on the first floor of the Palais de la Porte Dorée. Built for the 1931 Colonial Exhibition, this handsome building also houses the Musée de l'Histoire de l'Immigration.

Aquarium Tropical du Palais de la Porte Dorée
293 Avenue Daumesnil
75012 Paris
01 53 59 58 60
aquarium-tropical.fr

PIAF, SPARROW OR PASSERINE ?

The brown and gray plumage of **sparrows** looks a bit like a monk's habit. The word for monk, "moine", thus inspired the French term for these little birds, "moineau," which measure around 6 inches. In Paris, they're known colloquially as "piafs." This was the stage name adopted by the interwar years singer Édith Gassion, known as "**Môme Piaf**," whose waist was as slender as her voice was powerful.

BUTTERFLIES FLY AWAY

Not far from the Valley of Flowers and the herb beds, the Parc Floral boasts a 2,152-square-foot greenhouse where around 300 **butterflies** from 40 different species flutter about. Every week, between May 15 and October 15, the lepidopterans emerge from their chrysalises and grow among nettles and green plants, their favorite food.

Parc Floral de Paris
1 Route de la Pyramide
75012 Paris
01 49 57 25 50
parcfloraldeparis.com

PARADE HORSES

Chestnut, bay or grey, they patrol the Champs-Élysées every Wednesday before returning to the Célestins barracks' stables, home to the Republican Guard. The 140 **horses** of the cavalry regiment provide escorts for official honors, as well as surveillance of certain sites, such as stadiums, during major events.

Garde Républicaine
18 Boulevard Henri-IV
75004 Paris
01 58 28 20 99

WILD BEASTS

Mysterious and often shy, wild animals have their own place in Paris. Let's set off on an unusual safari adventure...

THE COMMON KESTREL: HIGH UP IN THE SKY

The kestrel is used to spotting its prey by soaring or even hovering in the air, using its own special technique. Since the 19th century, several pairs of these small birds of prey have nested every year in the towers of **Notre-Dame Cathedral and Saint-Sulpice Church**, without neglecting other tall buildings and monuments.

AS RELAXED AS WILD NEWTS

They spend their lives between the water and the shores of the pond in the **Jardin Naturel**, near Père-Lachaise. This garden, which has never undergone the slightest chemical treatment and has rarely seen a pair of pruning shears, was designed from the outset, in 1996, as a space for biodiversity where humans intervene as little as possible.

THEY DEVOUR EVERYTHING: CATFISH

Catfish can be found in the **Seine**, where they devour other fish, crustaceans and even coypu. This large fish can measure between 5 and 6.5 feet and weighs up to 110 pounds. But some of the monsters of this species have set new records: a catfish measuring 8.96 feet and 287 pounds was once caught in the Rhône river!

THE WELL-PROTECTED RED PANDA

Native to the Himalayas, it's the size of a small bear or a (very) large cat, and eats bamboo. This endangered species is one of the highlights of the **Menagerie at the Jardin des Plantes**. The "oldest zoo in the world," created during the French Revolution, is home to 200 species, a third of which are endangered.

WALKING IN THE YETI'S SHOES

The fossilized footprint of the "abominable snowman"—well, we imagine it's his... is preciously preserved among all manner of naturalized animals and fossils in **Deyrolle**'s cabinet of curiosities. Since 1831, this store, specializing in taxidermy and entomology, has been showcasing rare and spectacular items from the animal world.

THE ANIMAL CITY

Inside the **Parc Zoologique de Paris** you will find the largest number of wild animals: 245 species and over 2,000 animals are housed on this 37-acre site. Lions, jaguars, lynxes, rhinoceroses, primates, lemurs, snakes, sea lions... they all share five bio-zones recreating their natural environment as accurately as possible.

Jardin Naturel
120 Rue de la Réunion
75020 Paris
01 43 28 47 63

Ménagerie du Jardin des Plantes
57 Rue Cuvier
75005 Paris
01 40 79 56 01
jardindesplantesdeparis.fr

Parc Zoologique de Paris
Avenue Daumesnil
75012 Paris
0 811 22 41 22
parczoologiquedeparis.fr

Deyrolle
46 Rue du Bac
75007 Paris
01 42 22 30 07
deyrolle.com

SCARY CREATURES!

In Paris, some rather unsavory animals feed on our garbage and colonize the metro and underground spaces. But not all of them are pests...

NOT SO NICE PIGEONS

Paris' **tens of thousands of pigeons** are part of the cityscape, notably on the piazza in front of the Pompidou Center or the square at Notre-Dame. But the city doesn't do them much good: their life expectancy is three to four years, compared with more than twice that for pigeons on a farm. In any case, it's best not to think about roasting one on a spit for dinner: since they feed on polluted garbage, Parisian pigeons are highly toxic!

CITY RATS

In Paris, there are **two rats for every inhabitant**: that's around 4.5 million of these charming rodents that roam through Paris' cellars, parking lots, parks and sewers. Less foodie than the hero of the film *Ratatouille*, but still very greedy, they are particularly fond of the lawns opposite the Louvre, where tourists leave the remains of their picnics...

PIPISTRELLES IN DARK TUNNELS

On the former Petite Ceinture railway line, **1,500 pipistrelles**, the smallest of all bats, hibernate every year in a disused tunnel in the 14th arrondissement. This is the largest colony of this protected species in France.

COLONIES OF ROACHES...

Cockroaches are those charming little beasts that only come out in the kitchen at night to attack food and leave their various and assorted germs behind... Eugh!

METRO CRICKETS

Officially protected, **crickets** live on the ballast—the stones covering the ground between the rails of metro lines—where they enjoy ideal conditions: warmth between 80°F and 93°F and, above all, abundant food, consisting of sandwich crumbs and garbage thrown away by passengers. On lines 3 and 9, you can sometimes hear them singing, rather reminiscent of a vacation in the sun. But the gradual replacement of ballast with concrete is threatening their peaceful existence.

CELEBRITY ANIMALS

Certain animals have entered Paris' history. The first of their kind to be introduced in France, they aroused curiosity on their arrival or, associated with an event or an important person, they left a lasting impression.

PRASLIN, LOUIS XV'S RHINOCEROS

Captured in India at the request of Louis XV, this **rhinoceros** arrived in France in 1770 aboard the ship Duc de Praslin, from which it took its name. From Lorient, where he disembarked, he was taken by oxcart to the Menagerie de Versailles, where he proved to be aggressive and "very naughty." He died in 1793, during the Revolution, and his remains were naturalized for display at the Muséum National d'Histoire Naturelle.

MEDOR THE INCONSOLABLE

Médor, a loyal dog, stayed for days in front of the colonnade at the Louvre, where his master had died during the 1830 Revolution. Today, his name has become a symbol of the canine breed.

MARTIN, A FUNNY SORT OF BEAR

In 1820, people flocked to the very modern bear enclosure at the Jardin des Plantes, to laugh at the mischievous and ill-tempered **bear**, **Martin**. He was so famous that he bequeathed his name to all the menagerie's plantigrades, renamed Martin after him.

THE ELEPHANTS CASTOR AND POLLUX

Under the reign of Napoleon III, these **two Asian elephants** had pride of place at the Jardin des Plantes Menagerie. There were even rides on the elephants' backs organized around the park. But when the Prussians laid siege to Paris in 1870, the Parisians were so hungry that they slaughtered them to eat. It was only for a lack of anything better, as elephant meat is not generally considered a delicacy.

WHO'S THE TALLEST OF THEM ALL?

ZARAFA, THE CELEBRITY GIRAFFE

Born in Sudan, she was presented to King Charles X by the Pasha of Egypt in 1826. Once unloaded in Marseille, she walked 547 miles to Paris in 41 days. She was the first of her kind to set foot in France, and was naturally met with great enthusiasm. When she arrived at the Jardin des Plantes, hundreds of thousands of people flocked to see her. **Zarafa**, as she came to be known much later, triggered a real "giraffomania", inspiring fashion, hairstyles and interior decor. She died in 1845, then stuffed and exhibited at the Muséum de La Rochelle.

AND WHO IS THE HEAVIEST? LOL!

SIAM, THE ASIAN ELEPHANT

Star of Pierre Étaix's film *Yoyo* and a main attraction at the Vincennes Zoo, **Siam** died in 1997. He was stuffed using a new, more lifelike process, and can still be admired on the first level of the Grande Galerie de l'Évolution in the Muséum National d'Histoire Naturelle, away from the big parade of savannah animals.

STONE AND BRONZE LIONS

Not all lions are housed at the Vincennes zoo; many are in the city, with no bars or cages but standing as statues. They symbolize the virtues attributed to the king of the animal world: wisdom, power and courage. Let's go on a little urban safari.

THE LION OF THE REPUBLIC

Standing on the steps of the Marianne statue, in the middle of **Place de la République**, this bronze lion represents the power of universal suffrage, as indicated by the bronze plaque and ballot box behind it.

THE KING OF THE JUNGLE!

AND THE KING OF THE TOWN!

SO COOL...

THE DENFERT LION

He overlooks the square dedicated to Colonel Denfert-Rochereau, himself nicknamed "the lion" for his heroic resistance during the siege of Belfort in the 1870 war. The sculptor **Auguste Bartholdi**, who also created the Statue of Liberty, used the lion Brutus as his model, star of the Pezon Menagerie in Paris. He first created an enormous stone statue for the town of Belfort, then this one, which is a third of the size of the original.

THE LION FOUNTAIN

Not one but eight bronze lions guard the fountain on **Place Félix-Éboué**, by the metro station Daumesnil. This fountain, which used to be on Place de la République, was moved when the Marianne statue was erected.

A LA
DEFENSE NATIONALE
1870-1871

THE LIONS OF NUBIA

Two pairs of water-spouting lions bask on the edge of this fountain with basins, installed in front of the **Grande Halle de la Villette**. This is where the livestock from the covered market would come to quench their thirst. This fountain originally adorned the Place du Château-d'Eau (today's Place de la République).

LIONS AT HÔTEL DE VILLE

Two pairs of lions guard the entrances on the second facade of the Hôtel de Ville, rebuilt from 1874 onwards. The sculptor of one of the pairs, **Auguste Cain**, created virtually the same pair of lions for the monumental entrance to the town hall in Oran, Algeria, then a French colony.

THE FOUNTAIN, THE LION AND THE CROCODILE

Opposite the entrance to the Jardin des Plantes, on the corner of Rue Linné and Rue Cuvier, a sculpted fountain pays homage to the scientist **Georges Cuvier**, who studied animal anatomy. A young woman, representing natural history, is accompanied by an imposing lion and a magnificent crocodile. But the sculptor must not have been very well-versed in life sciences, as it's impossible for a crocodile to turn its head in the way his stone subject does.

THE LION GATE

On Quai des Tuileries, facing the Seine, two bronze lions protect the monumental porch leading to the Louvre's **Pavillon de Flore**. Behind the lions are the rooms devoted to the primitive arts. Next to the carrousel garden, some lionesses stand guard.

DELICIOUS FOOD IN PARIS

All the cuisines of the world are represented in Paris... but you can also try some real local specialties. Most of the time, you won't necessarily know they're from here.

THE BAGUETTE, AN INTERNATIONAL HIT

While the baguette's origins are not precisely known, its birthplace is undoubted. Parisian bakers supposedly invented it by changing the **recipe for Viennese bread**. Since the beginning of the 20th century, the long-shaped baguette with its white crumb has become a symbol of France.

THINGS ARE SERIOUSLY HEATING UP

Covered in grated gruyère cheese and melted under the grill, the "gratinée des Halles" is the Parisian version of **French onion soup**. Back in the day, it was eaten piping hot, early in the morning, by the Les Halles market sellers and partygoers ending their night out.

YUMMY HAM!

Long ago, there were numerous ham producers on the outskirts of Paris and they were well-known for their quality products. A slice of ham is a key ingredient in the famous "**jambon-beurre**," the most quintessentially Parisian sandwich.

DO "CHAMPIGNONS DE PARIS" STILL DESERVE THAT NAME?

The "Paris mushroom" originated in the capital, or more precisely, under it, since it was in the old **limestone quarries** on the Left Bank that its cultivation developed in the 19th century. Around 27 tons were harvested every day. The variety still exists, but the "Paris" mushroom is now grown... elsewhere. Mainly in Eastern Europe, and even in China!

Harvesting mushrooms in the underground quarries

The Duval Bouillon in the Parc du Champ-de-Mars, in 1878

LET'S ALL GO TO THE "BOUILLON"!

This word refers to a soup but also to a type of restaurant. In 1860, the butcher Pierre-Louis Duval created a bistro in the Les Halles district where he offered workers a hot and nourishing meat and vegetable soup which could be eaten quickly. Other Duval "bouillons" then popped up almost everywhere, only one of which has survived, now called the Brasserie Julien at 16 Rue du Faubourg-Saint-Denis. The idea was then adopted by the **Chartier** brothers. Their "bouillon" at 7 Rue du Faubourg-Montmartre hasn't changed since it opened in 1896.

Chez Chartier

PARISIAN DESSERTS

You can eat well in Paris–nobody will ever tell you otherwise. Especially if you're a pastry fan...

THE PARIS-BREST

Made from choux pastry, filled with pastry cream and covered in flaked almonds, this delicious cake is shaped like a wheel. It was created in 1910 by a pastry chef from Maisons-Laffitte, who was inspired by the Paris-Brest bike race.

THE OPÉRA

This sponge with coffee cream and chocolate frosting was created in Paris in the middle of the 20th century. Its name pays tribute to the apprentice dancers at the Opera House who frequented the patisserie.

THE SAINT-HONORÉ

Named after the patron saint of bakers and pastry chefs, this arrangement of cream-filled choux puffs covered in caramel was created around 1850 by the young chef Auguste Jullien, who was then employed. At the most famous patisserie of the time, Pâtisserie Chiboust.

THE TARTE BOURDALOUE

This tart with almond cream and pears owes its name to the street Rue Bourdaloue, opposite the Notre-Dame-de-Lorette church, where the pastry chef, who created the tart, was based in the mid-19th century.

THE MILLE-FEUILLE

With three layers of puff pastry alternated with pastry cream, this was the specialty of a pastry chef on Rue du Bac. The cake might have between 729 and 2,000 lamination layers, depending on the recipe.

THE BRIOCHE PARISIENNE

Its small head and rounded base—as opposed to the wide, elongated brioche from Vendée—and the delicacy of its light dough have made this brioche famous since the 17th century.

THE POIRE BELLE-HÉLÈNE

Pears poached in syrup covered in chocolate sauce: that's the recipe invented by the chef Auguste Escoffier in 1864 in tribute to the Offenbach opera, *La Belle Hélène*. Nowadays, we also add a scoop of vanilla ice cream.

THE FINANCIER

It was Lasne, a pastry chef based near the Paris stock exchange, who had the idea of shaping his "visitandines" (small almond cakes) to look like mini gold bars to appeal to his stockbroker and currency exchange customers.

THE PÊCHE MELBA

Decidedly inspired by singing, the same Escoffier, 30 years later, came up with a dessert for the opera singer Nellie Melba: peaches poached in vanilla syrup and topped with strawberry purée.

FEEDING THE PARISIANS

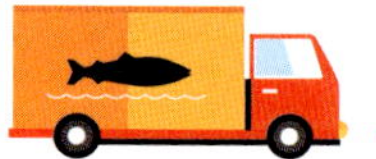

In order to feed Parisians (and the tourists that visit them), several hundreds of tons of produce is required every day. Before the railways and then cars were invented, these significant amounts were transported by carts on the roads or by boat along the Seine.

FROM THE RIVER TO HOUSEWIVES' BASKETS

Up until the 19th century, the Seine was the main commercial route in Paris. All kinds of food products were transported down the river, from wheat to wine, spices and other exotic products... not to mention firewood for kitchen stoves. The barges docked at various ports, the main one being the **Port de Grève**, in front of today's Hôtel de Ville.

"FAIRE GRÈVE," AN EXPRESSION THAT HAS CHANGED MEANING

On Place de Grève, unemployed workers would come every morning in the hopes of finding work unloading merchandise. Back then, the expression "**faire grève**" meant to look for work, not to go on strike like it does today.

Place de Grève in the Middle Ages

THE KINGS OF STRONG MEN

To transport the tons of merchandise to the Les Halles market, you had to be really strong! That was a job for the "**Les Halles strong men**," who you could recognize from their big yellow-leather hats, called "coltin," which were reinforced with lead on the inside so they could carry heavy loads on their heads and support their neck and shoulders.

The Les Halles strong men with their big hats

WHY IS RUE DES POISSONNIERS CALLED THAT?

From the north of Paris towards the center, Rues des Poissonniers, du Faubourg-Poissonnière and Poissonnière (all relating to fish, *poisson* in French) were part of the former **Chemin de la Marée (Tide's Way)**, which was used every night by carts arriving from the North Sea and Channel ports so they could deliver their cargo to the Les Halles market in the early hours of the morning.

Radishes! Who wants my radishhhhes?

THE BELLY OF PARIS

In the 19th century, the largest market was Les Halles, reserved for retailers who came to buy supplies for their stores. This "belly of Paris," as the novelist Émile Zola called it, was made up of several pavilions, each specialized in a particular type of product. It was a source of much nuisance right in the middle of Paris, and wasn't very practical, so the large **Les Halles market** was transferred to Rungis in 1969, and its pavilions were demolished in the years that followed.

GOING TO THE MARKET: AN ONGOING RITUAL

Every neighborhood has its own market, whether covered or not. Before domestic refrigerators became widespread in the 1950s, housewives shopped practically **every day**, as food could not be kept for very long.

The Les Halles market in the 19th century

In the fruit and vegetable pavilion

ROLL UP! ROLL UP! COME AND GET YOUR FRESH STRAWBERRIES!

YOU HAVE A PEACH OF MY HEART!

LEMONS! PUMPKINS! THEY'RE RIPE AND FRESH!

ORANGE YOU GLAD IT'S A BEAUTIFUL DAY?

IT'S ALL HAPPENING, UNDERGROUND

Sewers, quarries, catacombs... the Parisian underground is full of surprises! Beneath the city lies another one, with its own streets, its living and its dead. You can even visit certain districts...

EVERYTHING GOES TO THE SEWERS!

16 feet underground, 1,491 miles of pipes carry wastewater from Parisian homes out to the suburbs, where it is treated before being released into the Seine. The pipes follow the exact layout of Parisian streets. Designed under Napoleon III by the engineer **Belgrand**, this drainage network complemented the inadequate sewers that existed at the time. In the middle of the 19th century, many streets had not yet been rid of the foul-smelling streams that had been running through them... since the Middle Ages!

A tour of the sewers in the 19th century

AS HOLEY AS SWISS CHEESE!

Further down, 65 foot deep, lie 186 miles of underground tunnels. They, too, follow the course of the streets above ground. These tunnels were dug from the late 18th century onwards to search for the quarries from which the stones to build Parisian buildings had been extracted. As time went by, the city expanded... until it was built right on top of these old quarries, whose location was no longer precisely known. But building on top of a void is dangerous! That's why, after a few **collapses**, these tunnels were reinforced with walls strong enough to give the houses stable foundations.

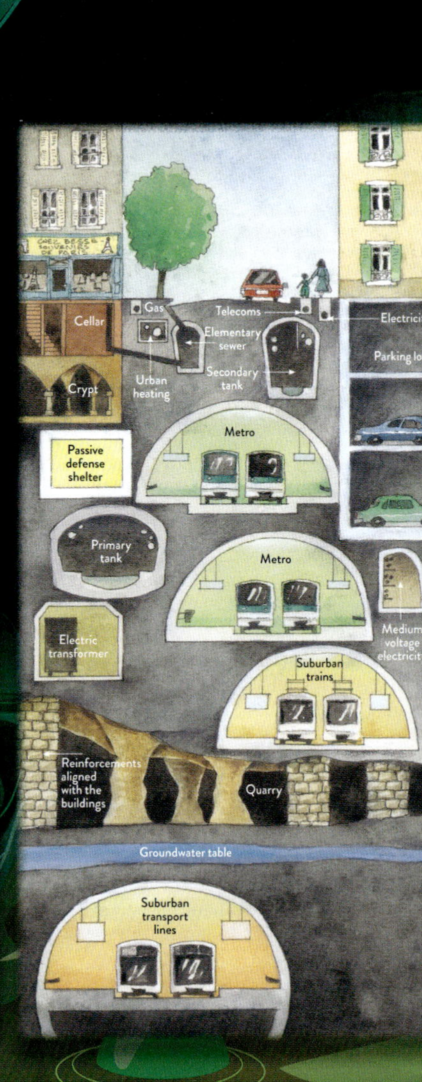

"...STOP, THIS IS THE EMPIRE OF DEATH"

This sign at the entrance to the **catacombs** may have been intended to frighten inquisitive visitors... but no coffins were ever actually deposited here. Between 1786 and 1814, these former quarries were used to store bones from Parisian cemeteries. The old cemeteries were emptied and closed at the same time as new, larger cemeteries were built outside the city limits (Père-Lachaise, Montparnasse, Montmartre...). So, in the catacombs the remains of six million Parisians were found, which the movers took care of arranging artistically, forming lines of skulls or hedges of shinbones.

Paris Catacombes
1 Avenue du Colonel-Henri-Rol-Tanguy
75014 Paris
catacombes.paris.fr

WHAT'S A "CATAPHILE"?

This word refers to people who like to venture into the quarries illegally to party or simply wander around. But these types of activities have been strictly forbidden since 1955, and the tunnels are patrolled by a police squad.

A former quarry under the Cochin Hospital

INCREDIBLE ACHIEVEMENTS

The capital and its monuments have been the setting for many world records. From the most astonishing to the most visionary, both on two wheels and on a tightrope.

5.6 MILES IN A HOT-AIR BALLOON

On August 27, 1783, a hydrogen-filled balloon designed by physicist Jacques Charles rose from the Champ-de-Mars and flew to Gonesse, in the north-western suburbs of Paris. The first manned flight took place on the following November 21, in a hot-air balloon with the scientist **Pilâtre de Rozier** on board, from Château de la Muette, near the Bois de Boulogne, to the Butte aux Cailles, in south Paris: 5.6 miles in 25 minutes.

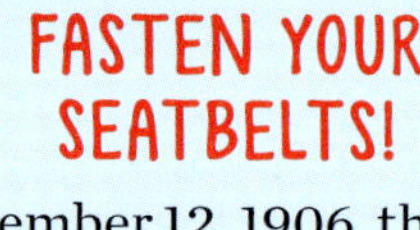

DRAISIENNE MADNESS

In 1818, in the Luxembourg gardens, 3,500 people attended the first demonstration of the **Draisienne**, named after its inventor Baron Drais. This velocipede, which did not yet have pedals, was so successful that a school and a Draisienne rental office opened next to the Parc Monceau.

FASTEN YOUR SEATBELTS!

On November 12, 1906, the aviator **Santos-Dumont** took off from the lawn at Bagatelle Park in his biplane, crossing 240 yards in 21 seconds at an altitude of 16 feet. It was the first flight in aviation history.

AN AIRPLANE ON THE GALERIES LAFAYETTE ROOFTOP!

The pilot **Jules Védrines**, a First World War hero, landed his biplane on the Parisian department store's roof in 1919. It was the first time a plane had landed on top of a building, which won the pilot a 25,000-franc prize... and a fine for having flown over Paris without a permit.

WALKING BETWEEN NOTRE-DAME'S TOWERS

In 1973, the tightrope walker **Philippe Petit** walked the distance between the cathedral's two towers on a wire stretched 216 feet above the ground. It was a preview of his display three years later, walking between the twin towers of the World Trade Center in New York.

MOUNTAINEERS CLIMB THE GRANDE ARCHE

The operation is carried out twice a year: harnessed like mountaineers, rope-access technicians scale the pillars of the Grande Arche de la Défense. Suspended in the void, these building acrobats clean the monument's glass surfaces!

ONE-OF-A-KIND COMPETITIONS

Paris is a sporting city! Not only because you can participate in all kinds of activities, but also because some competitions were created here or have become world famous.

Paulus, king swimmer

THE FIRST SWIM ACROSS PARIS

The first edition of this 7.5-mile race across the Seine took place on September 10, 1905. Eight swimmers started at the Pont National in Bercy, and only four reached the finish line at the Auteuil Viaduct. The winner, a Parisian shopkeeper named Paulus, completed the distance in 3 hours and 29 minutes. 50 years later, more than 300 swimmers, including some 50 women, took part in the event, before it was finally banned.

A RISKY BUSINESS, THE CAFÉ SERVERS' RACE!

This **legendary race** through the streets of Paris dates back to 1920. At a time when French-style service was highly reputed, it showcased the profession of café waiters. The rules: carry a tray loaded with glasses and bottles as quickly as possible from one spot to another. Without spilling anything, of course!

The café servers at the start of the race

THE PEDALLING "SQUIRRELS": THE SIX-DAY PARIS RACE

In the interwar years, this was the most famous cycling competition to take place at the Vélodrome d'Hiver, which was colloquially called the Vel' d'Hiv'. Each team would have two racers who would take turns doing a lap around the 820-foot track. They were nicknamed the "squirrels" because they didn't stop turning, like squirrels in a wheel. The best cyclists covered 2,175 to 2,485 miles in six days!

The Six Day racers

The sulkies, all wheels lined up...

FOR CHAMPIONS: THE PARIS MARATHON

26.2 miles. That's the compulsory distance of a marathon. This race, which is open to all, was first held in 1896, starting from Porte Maillot... before being organized again 80 years later, and every year since. Today, the start is on the Champs-Élysées and it ends on Avenue Foch... after a round trip to the Bois de Vincennes. The fastest runners complete the distance in 2 hours and 5 minutes!

OFF YOU TROT! THE PRIX D'AMÉRIQUE

On the last Sunday of every January since 1920, this prize has been awarded to the winner of a harness race in which the rider guides his horse from a lightweight carriage, called a **sulky**. This prestigious competition takes place at the Vincennes racecourse, considered the home of harness racing. The distance covered is 2,953 yards, which the champions cover in just over three minutes (the record, set in 2016, is 3 minutes 12 hundredths).

Marathon runners along the Seine

AND OFF WE GO! I'M GOING TO WIN THE TROPHY!

182

WHAT'S THAT FOR?

On our walks, we sometimes come across strange things. They seem even stranger when we wonder what purpose they might serve. Nowadays, they're pretty much useless... but that wasn't always the case.

This funny-looking **hook** curved like a corkscrew used to be for wrapping a rope around to lower or hoist up heavy items to and from the cellar through a basement window. Now that people store fewer sacks of coal or barrels in their basements, these hooks have practically all disappeared.

Before it became a public park, the Parc Monceau belonged to a nobleman. The landscaping he created evokes faraway lands: a Swiss farm, a Turkish tent, a Dutch windmill... Among other features, an **Egyptian pyramid** remains there.

This little house isn't a house at all, but a "**lookout post**" from which to inspect the underground pipes that carried water from Belleville to the center of Paris. The pipes could then be maintained or repaired.

42 Rue des Cascades

8 Rue des Grands-Augustins

This plaque is a **reference** indicating the altitude of a place in relation to the sea and the Seine. These measures were important when it came to installing the sewers, so that the slope would allow for drainage of wastewater.

13 Place Vendôme

OK, BUT HOW DO I MEASURE MYSELF?

During the French Revolution, it was decided that everyone would henceforth use the same unit of measurement: **the meter**. 16 plaques were installed around Paris. Only two remain: at 13 Place Vendôme and 85 Rue de Vaugirard.

This funny-looking machine was for warning the **fire department** when a fire broke out. They weren't so useful once everyone had a cell phone in their pocket! This is the last one visible in Paris.

The entrance porches of older buildings are often fitted with iron **bollards** or hoops. Their purpose? To protect walls and doors from the wheels of coaches and carriages.

THAT'S FOR ATTACHING MY BIKE OF COURSE!

85 Rue de Vaugirard

Along the roads, **kilometer markers** indicate the distance to the nearest town. It's still the case today... and it was in the past too. This one dates back to Gallo-Roman Paris.

In the 19th century, the most modern buildings were equipped with a gas supply for heating and lighting. Small **iron boxes** gave technicians access to the supply valves.

Cour de Rohan, 6th arrondissement

Before cars took over the roads, people got around on horseback. There were up to 80,000 horses in Paris. But how did people saddle up easily? By using this **step**, of course.

64,000

miles

are traveled every year by
the Eiffel Tower's elevators
(that's 2.5 times round the Earth)

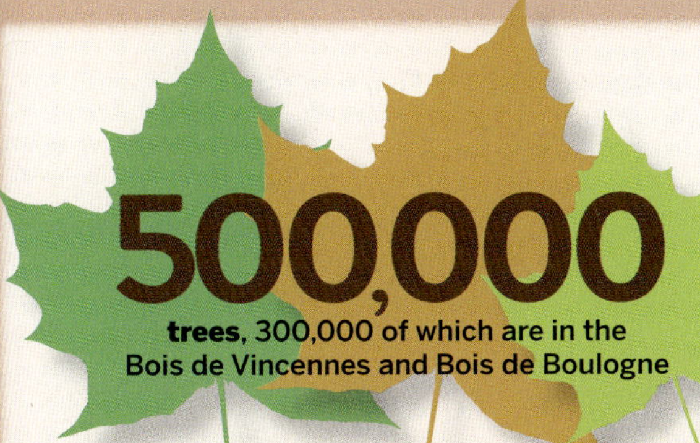

500,000

trees, 300,000 of which are in the Bois de Vincennes and Bois de Boulogne

7,000

days of **film shoots**, for 110 movies and 64 series in 2021

309
metro stations

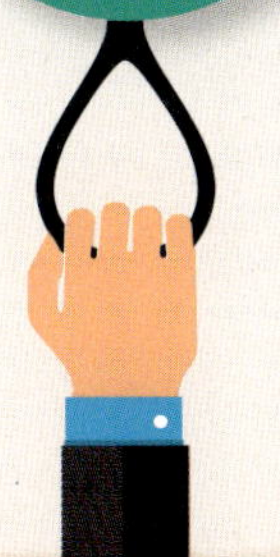

1,300

ANIMAL SPECIES

26

GALLONS OF DRINKING WATER
used on average
per person every day

171,000 STREET LAMPS

Parisians throw away

385

tons of cigarette butts
into the street per year

23,000
PIGEONS

133,000 TRAFFIC LIGHTS

Editorial direction: François Besse
Editorial coordination: Mathilde Kressmann
Translation from the French: Chloë Prestwich
Bilingual edit: Amy Collins
Artistic direction and design: Isabelle Chemin

Achevé d'imprimer en France en février 2024
sur les presses de l'imprimerie SEPEC - 12535231101

ISBN : 978-2-37395-242-1
Dépôt légal : mars 2024

Photographs and illustrations
© Coll. Parigramme, © Shutterstock et © Wikipedia Commons.